The Cross-Stitch Garden

The Cross-Stitch Garden

Melinda Coss

MEREDITH® PRESS
NEW YORK

For the "silly old tart"
and her
wonderful little tartlets

First published in Great Britain in 1995 by
Anaya, Collins & Brown Ltd, London

U.S. edition published by
Meredith® Press
150 E. 52nd Street
New York, NY 10022

Meredith® Press is an imprint of Meredith® Books:
President, Book Group: Joseph J. Ward
Vice-President, Editorial Director: Elizabeth P. Rice

Managing Editor: Jane Struthers
Design: Peartree Design Associates
Charts and Diagrams: Steve Dew and Delia Elliman
Photography: Jon Stewart
Jacket Photography: Di Lewis
Styling: Barbara Stewart

For Meredith® Press:
Executive Editor: Maryanne Bannon
Senior Editor: Carol Spier
Assistant Editor: Bonita M. Eckhaus
Technical Editor: Ellen W. Liberles

All correspondence should be addressed to Meredith® Press.

ISBN 0-696-20456-8
LOC 95-075766

Typeset in Great Britain by Bookworm Typesetting, Manchester
Color reproduction by Master Image, Singapore
Printed and bound in Singapore

Distributed by Meredith Corporation, Des Moines, Iowa

Contents

INTRODUCTION

There are two types of people in this world: those who can make their gardens grow and those who can't. As a rule, embroiderers fall into the first category. One particular stitcher I know has camellias that open on request. It's true, I've watched her. She talks to them very quietly and they open up their petals so they can hear her better. The result is a gloriously fragrant garden and a house full of intricately embroidered panels entitled "Camellias at dawn," "Camellias at midday," "Camellias at dusk" and so on.

Try as I might, I cannot make my garden grow. I choose plants carefully according to the conditions they require, I love them, I tend them, and I water them. What do they do in return? They shed their leaves and die. On one occasion in particular, I decided to grow a grapevine to ramble over the beams in my living room. The man at the nursery was extremely helpful and pointed me in the direction of a variety of dark (black) grape that promised me no problems. "Any idiot could grow this," he told me, so I bought it.

Two days later, my vine (now christened Harry) sat

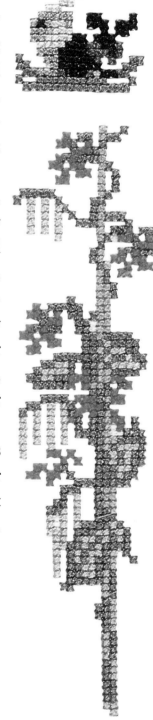

in a very grand Victorian jardinière in my cool but sunny studio. Three days after that, one leaf remained, flapping sadly halfway up the stem. In a fit of fury, I dumped the pot in my empty greenhouse and forgot about it. This year, two years after I bought him, Harry has suddenly burst into leaf. Why? Because he knows I'm not watching him.

One could get upset about these things, especially if, like me, you have a similar effect on machinery. My watch runs thirty minutes faster than everyone else's, and cars, washing machines and, dare I say it, computers, periodically look at me and throw themselves into a frenzy of inactivity. My publisher tells me it's because of my excessively creative energy levels, which is probably her polite way of saying I'm neurotic. But be that as it may, animals like me, children like me, and I still, no matter what, keep control over my needle and thread.

You do not have to have green fingers to enjoy this book. In fact, if you use it extensively, you could fill your house with flowers, fruit, vegetables, and wildlife without ever having to touch a trowel or get out the slug pellets.

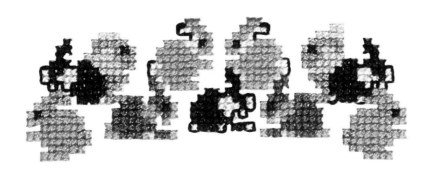

All you have to do is cross-stitch, and if you don't know how to do that, read the Techniques section at the back of this book before you begin. Cross-stitch is easy, I promise. The only point you have to remember is that all your top stitches must slant in the same direction. Once you have mastered the basic cross, there is no design in this book that is too complicated for you and, with the help of waste canvas, no fabric that cannot be cross-stitched. Your choice of project should be determined not by what you feel you are capable of doing, but by the time you have available to do it in.

In this book, as in my previous books, I have tried to give you a wide variety of uses for your finished work. If you are a beginner, I would suggest you start off with a project worked on 14-count Aida. This fabric is specially designed for cross-stitch and gives you clear holes so you can see where your needle has to go. When you have gained confidence, begin experimenting. Work the motifs on linen or on your shirt cuffs, and mix and match colored threads, incorporating metallic threads or beads as you go. Paint or stencil your background fabric to give a three-

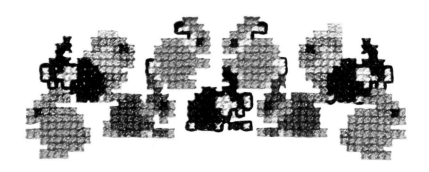

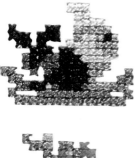

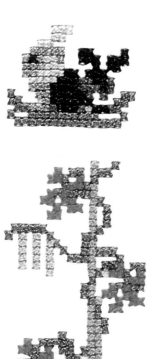

dimensional effect. All I am doing in this book is supplying you with some basic designs and my interpretation of them. The creative part should come from you – so do not be limited by my ideas.

When you have completely filled your house with needlework, start filling someone else's. Cross-stitch items make lovely gifts, gifts which show people that you have taken real time and trouble. I hope that I've included lots of ideas that will appeal to garden-lovers, for there is much more to gardens than just flowers. Even with its outstanding lack of cultivated plant life, my garden – which just happens to be a large meadow – overflows with wildflowers, herbs, brambles, rabbits, frogs, and squirrels, all of which I have interpreted in these pages.

Other stitchers gain pleasure from formal layouts, and some seasoned garden-lovers train their climbers into no end of unnatural positions. Whatever your taste in gardens, I hope you find something here that you will enjoy making and giving. Happy stitching!

MELINDA COSS

THE
ROSE GARDEN

Fashions in cross-stitch come and go but flowers always remain popular. I think that's because they're so beautiful and because they can be such a pleasure to stitch. It's also easy to find flowers that can act as your inspiration, whether it's winter or summer. Roses are among my favorite flowers, and I really enjoy designing with them. You can scatter tiny rosebuds over napkins, put them in corners of handkerchiefs, or stitch wonderfully large and full-blown roses on to pillows and tablecloths.

Jar of Roses

You can buy jars and pots in all kinds of materials, ranging from crystal to wood, from Framecraft (see Suppliers on page 166). These items have special lids in which you can enclose your cross-stitch design. For this tea rose stitched on linen, I have chosen a cut-glass jar. You could, of course, use this motif to brighten up a plain pillowcase or repeat it at random on a tablecloth.

Actual design measures: approximately 2¼ in (6 cm) square

Materials
1 piece of 32-count linen in ecru measuring 5 in (13.3 cm) square
No. 24 tapestry needle
1 Framecraft cut-glass jar with lid measuring 4 in (10 cm) in diameter – see page 166

DMC embroidery floss (cottons)

■ *1 skein of coral (351)*
□ *1 skein of peach (352)*
□ *1 skein of yellow (744)*
■ *1 skein of green (320)*
■ *1 skein of dark green (561)*
■ *1 skein of olive (832)*

Instructions
Mark the center of the chart and the center of the linen. Starting here, work in cross-stitch over two threads of the fabric using two strands of floss (cotton). When the design is complete, place it in the top of the jar according to the manufacturer's directions.

Stenciled Tablecloth and Napkins

The wonderful array of fabric paints and crayons that is available means you can now add to the dimensions of your needlework. To produce this design, I cut a rose pattern from a sheet of acetate, and stenciled petals and leaves onto an evenweave cloth. I then highlighted the images in cross-stitch using different shades of pink and green. Scatter the flower heads on your cloth at random and cross-stitch as many petals as you like.

Actual design measures:
About $4^3/_8 \times 4$ in (11×10 cm)

Materials
1 14-count evenweave tablecloth measuring approximately 34 in (86.4 cm) square
2 matching napkins
No. 24 tapestry needle
Tracing paper
Felt-tipped pen
Sheet of acetate
Craft knife
1 container of textile paint in bright pink
1 container of textile paint in bright green
Small stencil brush
Water

Instructions
Wash and iron the cloth to remove any sizing (dressing). With the tracing paper, trace the rose template with the felt-tipped pen. Place the acetate over your tracing and carefully cut out the shapes, as indicated on the template, with a craft knife to make a stencil.

Place the stencil on the cloth and paint through the holes (paint the petals in pink and the leaves in green). Repeat at random all over the cloth. Leave to dry and then heat set the colors, following the manufacturer's directions for the textile paint you are using. Following the chart for your color guide, work over the petal and leaf areas in cross-stitch using two strands of floss (cotton). Repeat the process for the napkins.

DMC embroidery floss (cottons)

1 skein of dark pink (602)

2 skeins of pink (957)

1 skein of green (3346)

1 skein of brownish-gray (535)

Textile paint in bright pink

Textile paint in bright green

Butterfly Pillow

There is nothing prettier than a huge down-filled, crisp white pillow, and there is now a wealth of Chinese cutwork and lace shams (covers) on the market. I have worked this butterfly motif on an extra-large sham for the garden room. If you can't find a suitable sham in your local linen store, check out the antiques shops or buy one by mail (see Suppliers on page 166).

Actual design measures:
7¼ × 4½ in (18.4 × 11.4 cm)

Materials
1 pillow sham (cover)
1 piece of 14-count waste canvas measuring 8½ × 6 in (21.6 × 15.2 cm)
No. 8 crewel needle
Sewing thread for basting
Sewing needle
Pair of tweezers

Instructions
Baste the waste canvas in position in the bottom right-hand corner on the front of the sham (cover). Take care not to stitch through both sides of the sham. Mark the center of the waste canvas and the center of the chart, and count out to the nearest stitch from this position. Starting here, work in cross-stitch using two strands of floss (cotton) until your design is complete. Remove the basting stitches, then pull the strands of waste canvas from under the embroidery with the tweezers.

DMC embroidery floss (cottons)

- 1 *skein of green (471)*
- 1 *skein of khaki (832)*
- 1 *skein of black (310)*
- 1 *skein of yellow (743)*
- 1 *skein of blue (792)*
- 1 *skein of red (349)*
- 1 *skein of gray (451)*
- 1 *skein of light violet (340)*
- 1 *skein of pink (224)*
- 1 *skein of beige (437)*
- 1 *skein of brown (801)*

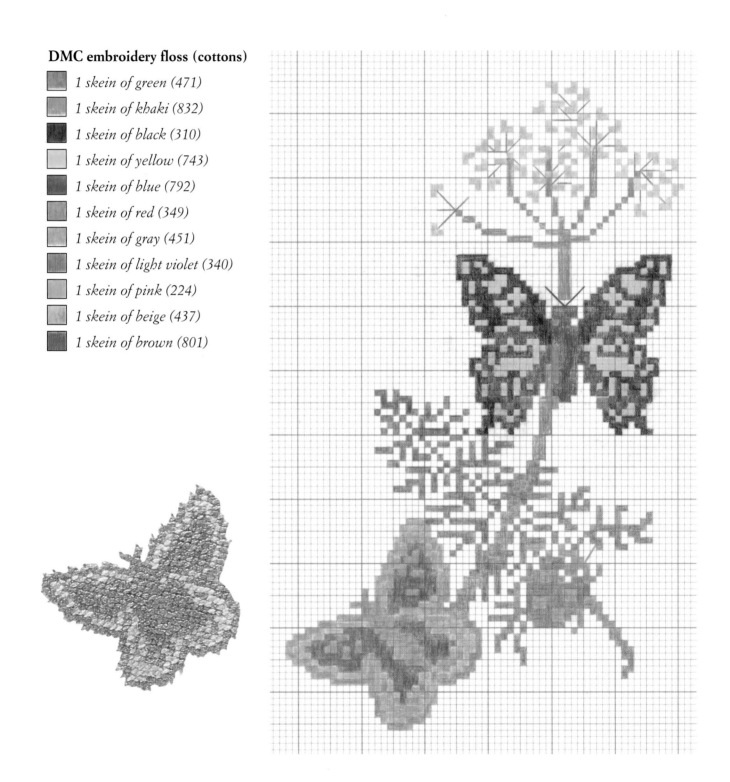

Roses on Checks Pillow

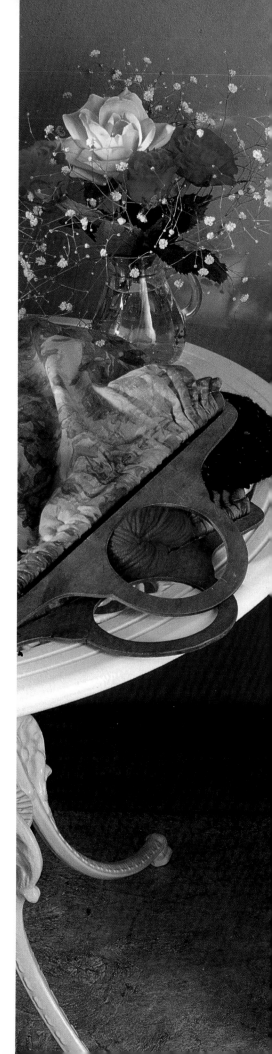

The shops are full of checked and striped cotton fabrics that are wonderfully useful to cross-stitchers. You can incorporate these patterns into your designs, using them as trellises on which to train your embroidered flowers. For this project I have chosen a Laura Ashley Windowpane Check fabric in green and worked the roses design using waste canvas (see Techniques on page 160). The final piece of work has been made into a pillow but you could make your own shades, tiebacks, or tablecloths.

Actual design measures:
7¾ in (19.7 cm) square

Materials

*1 piece of 14-count waste canvas
    measuring 10 in (25.4 cm)
    square*
No. 8 crewel needle
*1 piece of Laura Ashley
    Windowpane Check in green
    measuring 24 × 48 in
    (61 × 122 cm)*
Sewing thread for basting
*Sewing thread to match the
    checked fabric*
Sewing needle
Pair of tweezers
*Strip of Velcro™ measuring
    18 in (45.7 cm)*
Pins
Sewing machine
*Pillow form (pad) measuring
    16 in (40.6 cm) square*

Instructions

Cut out a piece of fabric measuring 20 in (50.8 cm) square. Baste the waste canvas into position on this piece of fabric, taking care to line it up properly with the vertical lines of the checked pattern and leaving a 6 in (15.2 cm) border at both edges. Find the center of the waste canvas and the center of the chart, and count out to the nearest stitch from this position. Starting here, work in cross-stitch using two strands of floss (cotton) until your design is complete. Carefully remove the basting stitches, then pull the strands of waste canvas from under the embroidery with the tweezers.

For the back, cut out two pieces of fabric, each measuring 11½ × 20 in (29.2 × 50.8 cm). With the wrong sides facing you, make a 1 in (2.5 cm) hem along one edge of each piece and iron it flat. Separate the two strips of Velcro and center the hooked one on the wrong side of one of the hems. Center the other piece of Velcro on the right side of the other hem. Neatly stitch over the ends of the Velcro to secure them. Now press the two pieces together so they form the back piece of the pillow.

Place the front and back pieces of the pillow cover with right sides together and pin the edges together. Machine-stitch around all four sides, with a ½ in (12 mm)

seam allowance. Turn the cover right side out and press the seams flat. Mark a stitching line around the back of the pillow, 2 in (5 cm) in from the outer edges. Work a row of hand or machine stitches along this line through the front and back of the pillow cover. Insert the pillow form.

DMC embroidery floss (cottons)

1 skein of olive (832)

1 skein of dark green (561)

2 skeins of green (562)

1 skein of peach (353)

1 skein of pink (3326)

1 skein of rose (335)

1 skein of dark rose (326)

Butterflies and Lace

Here is a collection of butterflies. Add one to a flower design or stitch them in a straight row to form a border for a mirror or picture frame. Work them on a linen panel, sampler-style, or do what I have done and incorporate them into a patchwork lace pillow. This pillow sham (cover) is hand-made in India and is available by mail (see Suppliers on page 166).

Actual designs measure: approximately 2 in (5 cm) square

Materials
1 patchwork lace pillow sham (cover) measuring 16 in (40.6 cm) square
No. 8 crewel needle
9 pieces of 14-count waste canvas, each measuring 3 in (7.6 cm) square
Sewing thread for basting
Sewing thread to match the pillow sham (cover)
Sewing needle
Pair of tweezers
Pillow form measuring 16 in (40.6 cm) square

Instructions
Carefully position and baste one waste canvas square to the center of each plain panel on the pillow sham (cover). Take care not to stitch through both sides of the sham. Mark the center of the canvas and the center of each chart. Starting here, work each motif in cross-stitch using two strands of

floss (cotton), except in the areas which are to be worked in white. Work these areas using one strand of white floss and one strand of Blending Filament. Work the stitches that are indicated on the chart as straight stitch using two strands of floss. Stitch designs 1 – 6 on the panels of the pillow sham. When these are complete, repeat designs 1 – 3 in the remaining panels. Carefully remove the basting stitches, then pull the strands of waste canvas from under the embroidery with the tweezers. Insert the pillow form.

DMC embroidery floss (cottons)

- *1 skein of light violet (340)*
- *1 skein of dark brown (3371)*
- *1 skein of cream (3047)*
- ・ *1 skein of white (blanc) plus 1 spool of Kreinik Metallics Blending Filament 093*
- *1 skein of green (320)*
- *1 skein of antique rose (223)*
- *1 skein of gray (451)*
- *1 skein of aqua (564)*
- *1 skein of copper (922)*
- *1 skein of light green (368)*
- *1 skein of gold (741)*
- *1 skein of tan (437)*
- *1 skein of red (817)*
- *1 skein of light blue (3325)*

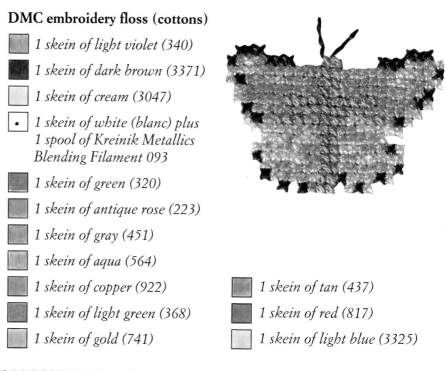

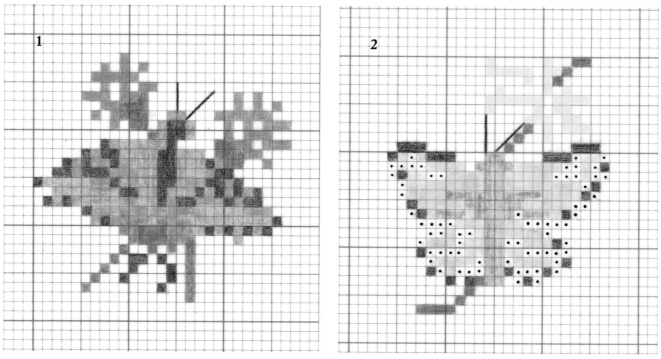

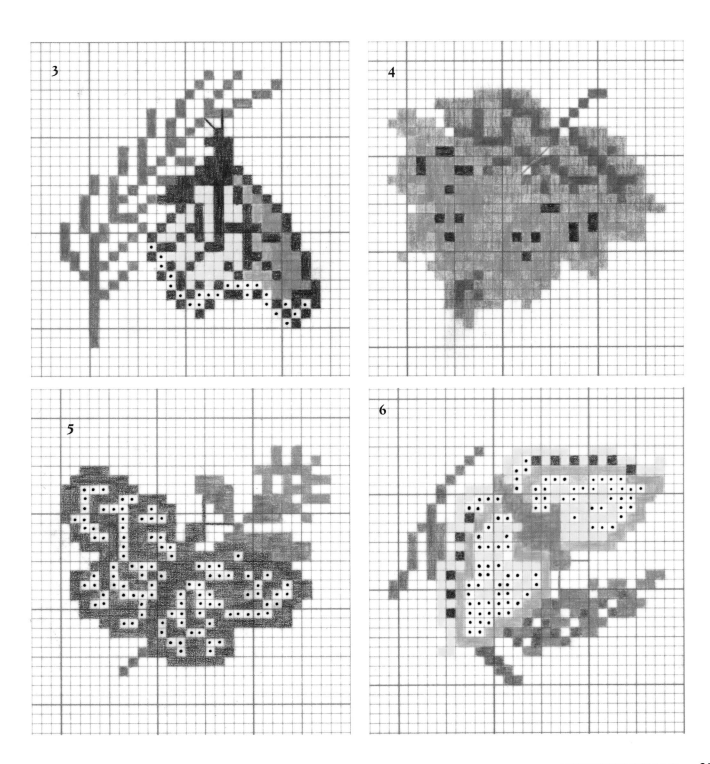

THE
PATIO

Patios provide a wonderful opportunity to garden without backbreaking toil, and many plants look good in pots. Geraniums are definitely among my favorite flowers, so I've made them the subject of a large pillow which I intend to use in the backyard on balmy afternoons. I have also come up with some miniature pictures. Remember that if you want to make them bigger, stitch the designs on a larger mesh canvas and increase the number of strands of thread you use accordingly.

Geranium Pillow

While this geranium design is aimed at those who prefer larger projects, the sham (cover) itself is simple to make and is the size of a pillow. You could also make a seat for an old-fashioned deck chair in the same cotton ticking or make a tablecloth incorporating a couple of the flower heads from the chart.

Actual design measures:
11⅛ × 20¾ in (28.3 × 52.7 cm)

Materials
1 piece of 14-count Zweigart
    Rustico measuring 24 × 16 in
    (61 × 40.6 cm)
No. 22 tapestry needle
1 piece of cotton ticking measuring
    48 × 28¼ in (122 × 71.7 cm)
Pins
Sewing machine
1 pillow

Instructions
Mark the center of the fabric and the center of the chart. Starting here, work in cross-stitch using three strands of floss (cotton) until the design is complete. Stitch a hem 2¾ in (7 cm) deep along each short edge of the ticking. Lay the ticking flat, right side up with the hemmed edges at top and bottom. Pin the finished design, positioned lengthwise across the ticking and centered between the hems, but with an extra ½ in (12 mm) of ticking at the top. Turning under the raw edges, stitch the design in place. With the ticking flat as before, fold first the bottom then the top hemmed edges toward the center, overlapping the edges by ½ in (12 mm). Pin the layers together along the side edges. Stitch the seams. Turn the finished sham (cover) right side out and press the seams flat. Insert the pillow.

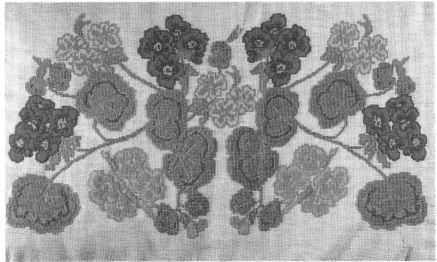

DMC embroidery floss (cottons)

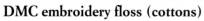 3 skeins of red (606)   2 skeins of bright pink (956)   1 skein of light coral (352)

3 skeins of dark red (817)   2 skeins of light pink (3708)   1 skein of brick (3721)

6 skeins of bright green (906) 1 skein of tan (437)

4 skeins of light green (907) 2 skeins of coral (351)

Little Watering Can

This little outdoor scene is one of a trio of mini-pictures. Just for good measure I've worked the watering can in Blending Filament (lurex) so it will catch the sun.

Actual design measures:
1⅝ × 2¼ in (4.1 × 5.7 cm)

Materials
*1 piece of 18-count Aida in cream
    measuring 5½ in (14 cm) square*
No. 25 tapestry needle
Your choice of frame

Little Flowerpots

DMC embroidery floss (cottons)

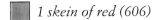 1 skein of red (606)

1 skein of yellow (444)

1 skein of gold (741)

1 skein of green (469)

1 skein of bright pink (956)

1 skein of blue (792)

1 skein of pale blue (794)

1 spool of Kreinik Metallics Fine Braid 001

1 skein of dark green (700) plus 1 spool of Kreinik Metallics Blending Filament 009

1 skein of light pink (3326)

Instructions

Mark the center of the Aida and the center of the chart. Starting here, work in cross-stitch using two strands of floss (cotton). Where Fine Braid is indicated, use two strands. When working in dark green, use one strand of floss and one strand of Blending Filament. Frame the design as you wish.

These two little flowerpots each take an evening to make and can be used either alone or to form a border. They also look great mounted as greeting cards.

Actual designs measure:
1¼ in (3.2 cm) square

Materials
2 pieces of 18-count Aida in cream, each measuring 5½ in (14 cm) square
No. 25 tapestry needle
Your choice of frame

Instructions

Mark the center of the Aida and the center of the chart. Starting here, work in cross-stitch using two strands of floss (cotton) until the design is complete. Frame the design as you wish.

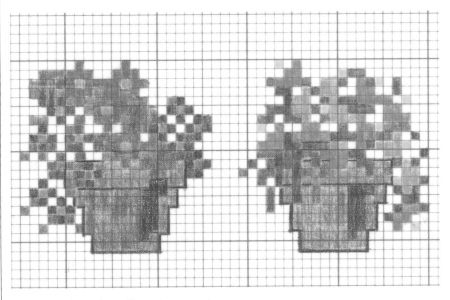

DMC embroidery floss (cottons)

1 skein of yellow (741)

1 skein of bright pink (956)

1 skein of light pink (3326)

1 skein of green (469)

1 skein of brown (632)

1 skein of terracotta (922)

1 skein of jade green (562)

1 skein of blue (792)

1 skein of red (606)

Backstitch in brown (632)

Flowerpots Hand Towel

This clever hand towel has an Aida border at both ends ready for you to stitch. I have used the flowerpots again, working this time on a lower count of Aida.

Actual design measures:
11¼ × 2½ in (28.6 × 6.3 cm)

Materials

1 Zwiegart Cottage Huck
   Towel with 8-count inserts
No. 20 tapestry needle

Instructions

Mark the center of the Aida at one end of the towel and the center of the chart. Starting here, work in cross-stitch using five strands of floss (cotton) until the design is complete. Repeat for the border at the other end of the towel. For a smaller hand towel as shown, trim at sides, then hem.

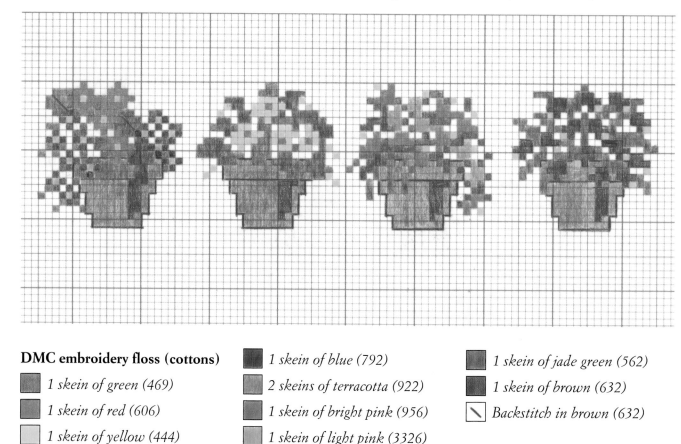

DMC embroidery floss (cottons)

- 1 skein of green (469)
- 1 skein of red (606)
- 1 skein of yellow (444)
- 1 skein of blue (792)
- 2 skeins of terracotta (922)
- 1 skein of bright pink (956)
- 1 skein of light pink (3326)
- 1 skein of jade green (562)
- 1 skein of brown (632)
- Backstitch in brown (632)

Crinoline Lady

No embroidery book can be complete without a lady sporting her crinoline, so I've cross-stitched this one on an oval tray cloth.

Actual design measures:
5⅛ × 7 in (13 × 17.8 cm)

Materials
1 piece of 14-count waste canvas
  measuring 6½ × 10¼ in
  (16.5 × 26 cm)
No. 8 crewel needle
1 oval lace-trimmed tray cloth
  —see Suppliers on page 166
Sewing thread for basting
Sewing needle
Pair of tweezers

Instructions
Position the waste canvas in the center of the tray cloth and baste in place. Mark the center of the canvas and the center of the chart. Starting here, work in cross-stitch using two strands of floss (cotton) until the design is complete. Carefully remove the basting stitches, then pull the strands of waste canvas from under the embroidery with the tweezers.

DMC embroidery floss (cottons)

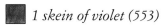 *1 skein of lilac (554)*

1 skein of violet (553)

1 skein of fuchsia (602)

1 skein of old gold (729)

1 skein of yellow (743)

1 skein of light blue (794)

1 skein of dark blue (792)

1 skein of green (907)

1 skein of cream (951)

Little Bee Box

If you like sweets, why not make yourself a little bee box to keep mints or candies in? This bee has a habit of including herself in many of my garden designs. I wonder why?

Actual design measures: about ¾ in (18 mm) square

Materials

1 piece of 32-count linen in ecru measuring 4 in (10 cm) square
No. 24 tapestry needle
1 Framecraft pillbox – see Suppliers on page 166

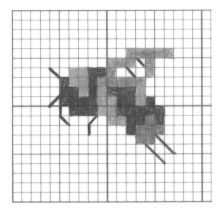

DMC embroidery floss (cottons)

■ *1 skein of brown (801)*
■ *1 skein of mustard (729)*
■ *1 skein of gold (742)*
■ *1 skein of mushroom (3042) plus 1 spool of Kreinik Metallics Blending Filament 002*

Instructions

Mark the center of the chart and the center of the fabric. Starting here, work in cross-stitch using two strands of floss (cotton) over two threads of linen. When using the mushroom floss, use one strand of mushroom and one strand of Blending Filament. Work the backstitch areas using two strands of brown floss. When the design is complete, mount it in the pillbox lid following the manufacturer's directions.

Violets, Primroses, and Bluebells

These flowers welcome in the spring, and domesticated varieties sit in pots decorating our homes and windowsills. With the help of waste canvas, I have scattered some flowers over a beautiful white cutwork tablecloth available by mail. You may have other ideas for them.

Central panel design measures:
5¾ × 6 in (14.6 × 15.2 cm)
Small motifs measure:
2 × 2¼ in (5 × 5.7 cm)

Materials
*1 piece of 14-count waste canvas
    measuring 8 in (20.3 cm) square*
*4 pieces of 14-count waste canvas
    measuring 3 in (7.6 cm) square*
No. 8 crewel needle
*1 cutwork tablecloth – see
    Suppliers on page 166*
Sewing thread for basting
Sewing needle
Pair of tweezers

Instructions
Center the large piece of waste canvas on the tablecloth and baste in position. Place the four smaller

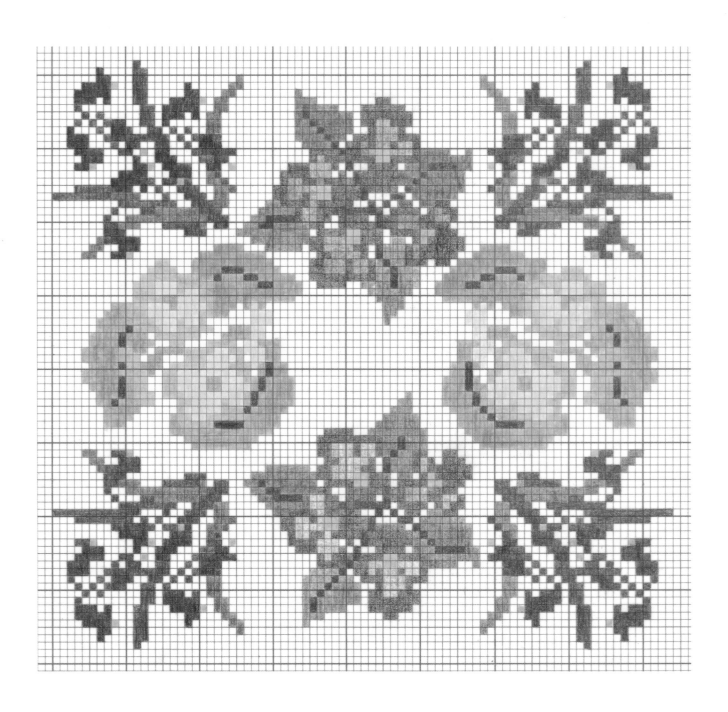

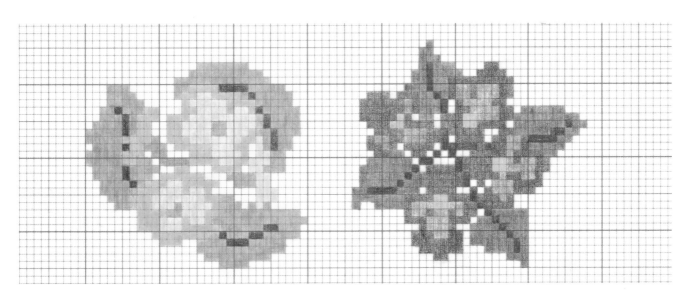

pieces in position at the four corners. To work each design, mark the center of the canvas and the center of the chart. Starting here, work in cross-stitch using two strands of floss (cotton) until each design is complete. Remove the basting stitches, then pull the strands of waste canvas from under the embroidery with the tweezers.

DMC embroidery floss (cottons)

1 skein of green (906)

1 skein of blue (792)

1 skein of yellow (972)

1 skein of light yellow (727)

1 skein of light green (3347)

1 skein of dark green (561)

1 skein of purple (553)

1 skein of dark purple (550)

HERBS AND WILDFLOWERS

From time immemorial, herbs have cured us, comforted us, and added aroma and flavoring to our culinary efforts. They are grown with pride in formal herb gardens and with ingenuity among the rocky nooks and crannies of our town and country backyards. Herbs sit decoratively in pots, on shiny countertops, or neatly in window boxes below the kitchen window. Dry them and hang them in bunches for their fragrance. Stuff them into sachets, or create stitched images to hang on your walls.

Portrait of Rosemary

For this project I have chosen shimmery Zweigart Damask Aida. I have also mixed Blending Filament with matte cotton Flower Threads to create the atmosphere of a dewy morning. Wrapping fabric around a picture mat gives your finished embroidery a unique style which you can coordinate with your furnishings. This idea works particularly well in a wood kitchen or a sunroom. These herbal pictures would be charming also as pillows, apron bibs, or album covers.

Actual design measures:
10¼ × 8¼ in (26 × 21 cm)

Materials

1 piece of 18-count Zweigart Damask Aida in ivory measuring 14 × 13 in (36 × 33 cm)
No. 25 tapestry needle
1 piece of cotton fabric measuring 20 in (50.8 cm) square
1 piece of acid-free cardboard measuring 13 × 12 in (33 × 30.5 cm)
1 piece of acid-free mat (mounting) board measuring 16 × 14¾ in (40.6 × 37.5 cm) with a central cut-out area measuring 11 × 9½ in (28 × 24.1 cm)
Rubber cement (glue)

Instructions

Mark the center of the chart and the center of the Aida. Starting here, work in cross-stitch using two strands of Flower Thread. Where Blending Filament is listed, use one strand of Flower Thread and one strand of Blending Filament. Where straight stitch is indicated, use one strand of Flower Thread only. When the design is complete, mount it on the acid-free cardboard, using rubber cement (glue) and keeping fabric threads straight. Center the mat (mounting) board on the wrong side of the cotton fabric and glue the edges of the fabric to the back of the board. Turn right side up and cut a corner-to-corner cross in the fabric covering the center opening. Trim the fabric points to leave a 1¼ in (3.2 cm) flap at each edge. Fold these flaps to the back of the mat board and glue in place. Center and glue the fabric-covered mat on the front of your needlework and frame as you wish.

DMC Flower Threads

- 1 skein of light green (2369)
- 1 skein of mauve (2916)
- 1 skein of pink (2778) plus 1 spool of Kreinik Metallics Blending Filament 013
- 1 skein of white (blanc) plus 1 spool of Kreinik Metallics Blending Filament 023
- 1 skein of gray (2280) plus 1 spool of Kreinik Metallics Blending Filament 001
- 3 skeins of dark green (2320)
- 1 skein of dusty plum (2724)
- Straight stitch in dark green (2320)

Sage in Pine

Here is a sister for Rosemary. I've emphasized the silvery quality of sage leaves with metallic thread, and once again I've used shimmery Damask Aida. You could turn these designs into herb bags or pillows, or work them on a lower count of canvas, which will make them larger and quicker to complete.

Actual design measures:
10¼ × 8¼ in (26 × 21 cm)

Materials
*1 piece of 18-count Zweigart
   Damask Aida in ivory measuring
   14 × 13 in (36 × 33 cm)
No. 25 tapestry needle
1 piece of cotton fabric measuring
   20 in (50.8 cm) square
1 piece of acid-free cardboard
   measuring 13 × 12 in
   (33 × 30.5 cm)
1 piece of acid-free mat (mounting)
   board measuring 16 × 14¾ in
   (40.6 × 37.5 cm) with a central
   cut-out area measuring
   11 × 9½ in (28 × 24.1 cm)
Rubber cement (glue)*

Instructions
Mark the center of the chart and the center of the Aida. Starting here, work in cross-stitch using two strands of Flower Thread. Where Blending Filament is listed, use one strand of Flower Thread and one strand of Blending Filament. Where Balger Cord is listed, use one strand of Flower Thread and one strand of Balger Cord. Where straight stitch is indicated, use one strand of Flower Thread only. When the design is complete, stretch and mount it on the cardboard, gluing the edges to the back with rubber cement (glue). Cover the piece of mat board with the cotton fabric (see page 50) and frame it.

DMC Flower Threads

☐ *1 skein of gray (2415) plus
1 spool of Kreinik Metallics
Blending Filament 041*

▨ *2 skeins of green (2320)*

▨ *1 skein of mauve (2395) plus
1 spool of Kreinik Metallics
Balger Cord 012C*

▨ *1 skein of lilac (2396) plus
1 spool of Kreinik Metallics
Balger Cord 007C*

▨ *3 skeins of light green (2369)*

▨ *1 skein of antique rose (2329)*

▨ *1 skein of donkey brown
(2241)*

◩ *Straight stitch in dark green
(2320)*

Chickory Dishtowel

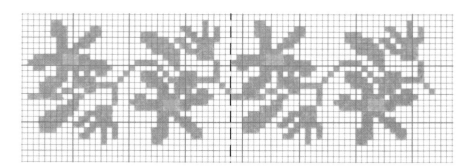

This design features chickory flowers. You can braise chickory, roast it, use it as a coffee substitute, or blanch the leaves and young shoots and toss them in a salad. For this project I used a special towel woven with an Aida band ready for you to embroider. You can achieve a similar result by stitching an embroidered Aida band to any towel.

Actual design measures:
4¼ × 2¾ in (10.7 × 7 cm)

Materials
1 Zweigart Cottage Huck Towel
with 8-count inserts
No. 20 tapestry needle
Sewing thread to match the fabric
Sewing needle

DMC embroidery floss (cottons)

- *3 skeins of blue (794)*
- *2 skeins of green (3348)*
- *1 skein of pink (3326)*

Instructions
Find and mark the center of the Aida at one end of the towel and the center of one motif (two repeats of the motif are shown on the chart, one on each side of the broken line). Starting here, work the motif in cross-stitch using five strands of floss (cotton). When the motif is complete, repeat it twice more as shown in the photograph. Work the opposite border in the same way.

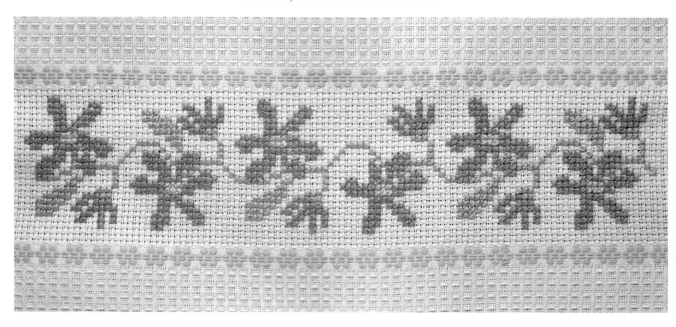

Sweetheart

This little heart could be filled with potpourri and hung on the bathtub faucet (tap). You could also use these hearts as seed packs. Cross-stitch a flower head and the name of the flower on the front of the heart, stitch the two halves of the heart together, and unzip the back of the heart to insert the seeds. Hearts make lovely gifts for all sorts of occasions.

Actual design measures:
2½ in (6.4 cm) square

Materials

1 piece of 14-count waste canvas measuring 4 in (10 cm) square
1 lace heart – see Suppliers on page 166, or make your own, using linen scraps, lace trim, and a small zipper
No. 8 crewel needle
Sewing thread to match lace heart
Sewing thread for basting
Sewing needle
Pair of tweezers
Potpourri

DMC Flower Threads

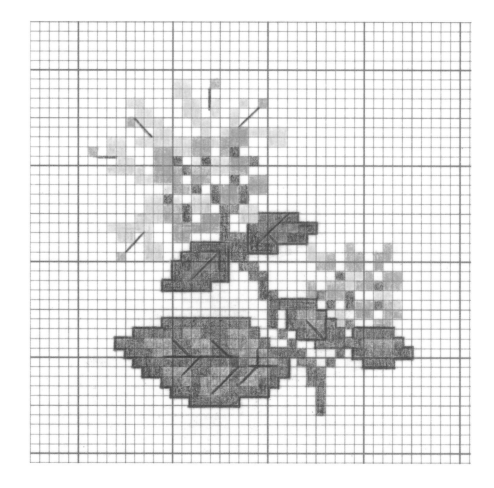

1 skein of pink (2776) plus
1 spool of Kreinik Metallics
Blending Filament 092

1 skein of light pink (2818)
plus 1 spool of Kreinik Metallics
Blending Filament 100

1 skein of dark green (2319)

1 skein of green (2320)

1 skein of gray (2241)

Instructions

Use a purchased heart, or make your own by cutting two fabric hearts, inserting a zipper on one, and edging the other with lace. Baste the waste canvas onto the center of the front half of the heart. Mark the center of the chart and the center of the canvas. Starting here, work in cross-stitch using two strands of Flower Thread. Where Blending Filament is listed, use one strand of Flower Thread and one strand of Blending Filament. Use one strand of Flower Thread only for straight stitch. When the design is complete, carefully remove the basting stitches, then pull the strands of waste canvas from under the embroidery with the tweezers. Neatly sew the two halves of the heart together around the outside edge. Unzip the back of the heart, fill it with potpourri, and rezip.

Wise Heart

This wise old lace heart should be filled with potpourri and hung in your wardrobe. Sachets make lovely gifts, and you can stitch them using many of the motifs in this book. When you buy these little hearts, they are supplied in two halves, so you can work your embroidery using waste canvas and then stitch the back and front pieces together.

Actual design measures:
2½ in (6.4 cm) square

Materials

1 piece of 14-count waste canvas
    measuring 4 in (10 cm) square
1 lace heart – see Suppliers on
    page 166 – or make your own
No. 8 crewel needle
Sewing thread to match
    lace heart
Sewing thread for basting
Sewing needle
Pair of tweezers
Potpourri

Instructions

Use a purchased heart, or make your own by cutting two fabric hearts, inserting a zipper on one and edging the other with lace. Baste the waste canvas onto the center of the front half of the heart. Mark the center of the chart and the center of the canvas. Starting here, work in cross-stitch using two strands of Flower Thread. Where Blending Filament is listed, use one strand of Flower Thread and one strand of Blending

Filament. Where Balger Cord is listed, use one strand of Flower Thread and one strand of Balger Cord. Use one strand of Flower Thread only for straight stitch. When the design is complete, carefully remove the basting stitches, then pull the strands of waste canvas from under the embroidery with the tweezers. Neatly sew the two halves of the heart together around the outside edge. Open the zipper at the back of the heart, fill with potpourri, and rezip.

DMC Flower Threads

■ *1 skein of mauve (2395) plus 1 spool of Kreinik Metallics Balger Cord 012C*

■ *1 skein of lilac (2396) plus 1 spool of Kreinik Metallics Balger Cord 007C*

■ *1 skein of antique rose (2329)*

■ *1 skein of light green (2369)*

■ *1 skein of green (2320)*

■ *1 skein of gray (2415) plus 1 spool of Kreinik Metallics Blending Filament 041*

■ *1 skein of donkey brown (2241)*

Floral Clock

The flowers for this clock were picked from the hedge. Wild roses, bluebells, and violets, among other wildflowers, surround the clock face in abundance. I have used a brass clock face which you can order by mail (see Suppliers on page 166) but, if you are feeling ambitious, you could chart and stitch your own clock face numbers on the fabric and then insert a quartz clock movement and set of hands.

Actual design measures:
About 11 in (28 cm) square

Materials
*1 piece of 14-count Aida in white
    measuring 15½ in (39.4 cm)
    square*
No. 22 tapestry needle
*Clock face measuring 5 in
    (12.7 cm) in diameter – see
    Suppliers on page 166*
*Quartz clock movement and hands
    – see Suppliers on page 166*
*1 piece of acid-free mat (mounting)
    board measuring
    11 in (28 cm) square*
Rubber cement (glue)
Knitting needle

DMC embroidery floss (cottons)

-  1 skein of light yellow (727)
- 1 skein of rose (224)
- 1 skein of pink (754)
- 1 skein of dark rose (223)
- 1 skein of yellow (972)
- 1 skein of cream (677)
- 1 skein of dark green (580)
- 2 skeins of green (3364)
- 1 skein of purple (552)
- 1 skein of light purple (554)
- 1 skein of fuchsia (602)
- 1 skein of blue (794)
- 1 skein of olive (834)

Instructions

Mark the center of the chart and the center of the Aida. Count out from this point to the nearest flower and begin stitching here. Work the design in cross-stitch using three strands of floss (cotton). When the design is complete, stretch and mount it on the mat board, gluing the edges to the back with rubber cement. Find the center of the design and use the knitting needle to make a hole through the Aida and mat board. Glue the clock face in position and, when it is dry, insert the quartz movement and the hands, following the manufacturer's directions.

Sweet Marjoram Bolster

Sweet marjoram has delicate pretty pink flowers and, when brewed as a tea, relieves the symptoms of bronchitis and colds. It also calms the nerves and helps to combat stress.

Actual design measures:
10¼ × 8½ in (26 × 21.6 cm)

Materials

1 piece of 18-count Aida in ecru measuring 24 × 13 in (61 × 33 cm)
No. 25 tapestry needle
2 pieces of cotton fabric each measuring 12½ × 24 in (31.7 × 61 cm)
1⅛ yards (1 meter) cord
1 bolster form or roll of batting (wadding) measuring 20 in (51 cm) long × 8 in (22 cm) diameter

DMC Flower Threads

1 skein of gray (2241)

3 skeins of dark green (2319)

1 skein of green (2320)

1 skein of pink (2776) plus 1 spool of Kreinik Metallics Blending Filament 092

1 skein of light pink (2818) plus 1 spool of Kreinik Metallics Blending Filament 100

1 skein of yellow (2748)

1 skein of light yellow (2743)

Instructions

Mark the center of the chart and the center of the Aida. Starting here, work in cross-stitch using two strands of Flower Thread. Where Blending Filament is listed, use one strand of Flower Thread and one strand of Blending Filament. Use one strand of Flower Thread for straight stitch only. Stitch a cotton piece to each long side of embroidered Aida to form a panel 24 × 36 in (61 × 91.4 cm) with the design at the center. Make a 1½ in (3.8 cm) hem along each short edge. With right sides together, fold the piece in half crosswise and seam the long edges together between the hems. Insert a bolster form or roll of batting (wadding). Thread cord through each hem, pull to gather and tie.

THE ORCHARD

This collection of designs, based on fruits and berries, provided the inspiration for this book. The very first design I produced was the Fruit Mirror on page 77. I sent it for stitching to Carolyn Palmer, who is the most excellent of stitchers. Having worked poor Carolyn to the bone, I decided that, for general consumption, the fruit on the mirror should be extracted and included in smaller projects. I hope you will agree that the finished project looks stunning. If you like a challenge, have a go!

Adam and Eve Barometer

The Garden of Eden can get steamy, so it is best to check the temperature there from time to time. The barometer kit is available by mail and, of course, you could use a clock face if you prefer. I had this design professionally mounted and framed, but if you are handy with a craft knife, there is no reason why you shouldn't do it yourself.

Actual design measures:
16 × 11¾ in (40.6 × 29.9 cm)

Materials

1 piece of 11-count Aida in cream
*   measuring 19½ × 15 in*
*   (49.5 × 38.1 cm)*
No. 22 tapestry needle
1 barometer measuring 5½ in
*   (14 cm) in diameter (see*
*   Suppliers on page 166)*
1 piece of heavyweight acid-free
*   cardboard measuring*
*   17 × 12¾ in (43.2 × 32.4 cm)*
Craft knife
Rubber cement (glue)
Your choice of frame

DMC embroidery floss (cottons)

- 1 skein of brown (839)
- 2 skeins of light brown (433)
- 1 skein of red (666)
- 1 skein of yellow (725)
- 2 skeins of green (469)
- 1 skein of pink (602)
- 1 skein of lime green (907)
- 1 skein of blue (794)
- 1 skein of light peach (754)
- Straight stitch in gray (535)

Instructions

Mark the center of the chart and the center of the Aida. Count out from here to the nearest stitch. Starting here, work in cross-stitch using three strands of floss (cotton) until the design is complete. Position the barometer on the cardboard and draw a circle the same size as the whole barometer (not the face), so the barometer fits comfortably in the hole. Remove the barometer and stretch your finished design over the cardboard, gluing the raw edges to the back. Cut a cross over the hole and trim the resulting triangles, leaving a margin about 1 in (2.5 cm) deep. Clip at intervals and fold the excess through the hole, gluing to the back of the cardboard. Leave to dry. Frame the finished embroidery as you wish, inserting the barometer through the hole.

Pair of Pears

This panel could be used as a wallhanging, a framed picture, or a runner. Or, you could work the pears along one edge of some 14-count fabric and finish it as a placemat. The design works particularly well in a traditional setting.

Actual design measures:
17 × 8½ in (43.2 × 21.6 cm)

Materials
*1 piece of 11-count Aida in cream
    measuring 22 × 12 in
    (55.9 × 30.5 cm)*
No. 22 tapestry needle

DMC embroidery floss (cottons)

1 skein of copper (922)

1 skein of light olive (834)

1 skein of brown (632)

1 skein of straw (676)

2 skeins of olive (832)

1 skein of yellow (972)

2 skeins of dark green (367)

2 skeins of light green (3347)

2 skeins of gray (415)

1 skein of pink (3716)

• 2 skeins of white (blanc)

Instructions

Mark the center of the chart and the center of the Aida. Starting here, work in cross-stitch using three strands of floss (cotton). Work the details on the bee in backstitch using two strands of brown. When the design is complete, carefully unravel the edges of the Aida to form a fringed border.

Fruit Mirror

This design is not for the faint-hearted, but if you have the courage to work it, please get a professional framer to make it into a mirror for you. After all the work it involves, the Fruit Mirror deserves the very best finish. For those with a very handy person at home, I am giving you the dimensions of the mat (mounting) board but I really wouldn't recommend doing it yourself.

Actual design measures:
$21\frac{1}{4} \times 30$ in (54×76.2 cm)

Materials

1 piece of 16-count Aida in summer khaki measuring $26\frac{1}{2} \times 34$ in (67.3×86.4 cm)
No. 24 tapestry needle
1 piece of acid-free mat (mounting) board measuring $22\frac{1}{4} \times 31$ in (56.5×78.7 cm)
1 piece of synthetic batting (wadding) measuring $22\frac{1}{4} \times 31$ in (56.5×78.7 cm)
1 mirror measuring approximately 13×19 in (33×48.2 cm)
1 piece of masonite (hardboard) measuring $22\frac{1}{4} \times 31$ in (56.5×78.7 cm)
Rubber cement (glue)
Strong general-purpose glue
Craft knife

Instructions

Photocopy the individual charts and, using the placement chart as a guide, tape them together (you will need reverse copies of several

of the charts). Mark the center of your placement chart and the center of the canvas. Count out from here to the nearest stitch and, starting here, work in cross stitch using two strands of floss (cotton) until the design is complete. Work the upper left section first, then the upper right section, the lower right section and, finally the lower left section. Cut out the center of the mat (mounting) board, leaving a border measuring 7 in (17.8 cm). Cut the batting (wadding) to fit over the frame and glue into position using the rubber cement (glue). Leave to dry. Stretch the completed work over the padded board and glue the raw edges to the back with the rubber cement. Cut a corner-to-corner cross on the center panel of the Aida and trim the excess canvas, leaving a margin of 1 in (2.5 cm). Fold this through the frame, carefully slitting the corners to make a neat edge, and glue it to the back with the rubber cement. Glue the mirror into position on the piece of masonite (hardboard) using the strong general-purpose glue. Glue the frame to the masonite, again using the strong general-purpose glue. If desired, glue a length of cord around the inner edge.

The individual charts for the separate items featured in the Fruit Mirror are given on the following pages. The amount of floss specified is for the whole project. The diagram here shows how these items are arranged around the mirror's border. One square equals 1 cm.

DMC embroidery floss (cottons)

- · 4 skeins of white (blanc)
- 2 skeins of copper (922)
- 2 skeins of straw (676)
- 2 skeins of light olive (834)
- 3 skeins of gray (415)
- 4 skeins of olive (832)
- 3 skeins of violet (333)
- 2 skeins of plum (3721)
- 4 skeins of purple (550)
- 3 skeins of bright yellow (972)
- 3 skeins of light pink (3716)
- 3 skeins of dark rose (309)
- 3 skeins of brown (801)
- 3 skeins of red (666)
- 5 skeins of green (3347)
- 12 skeins of dark green (367)
- 1 skein of lime green (472)

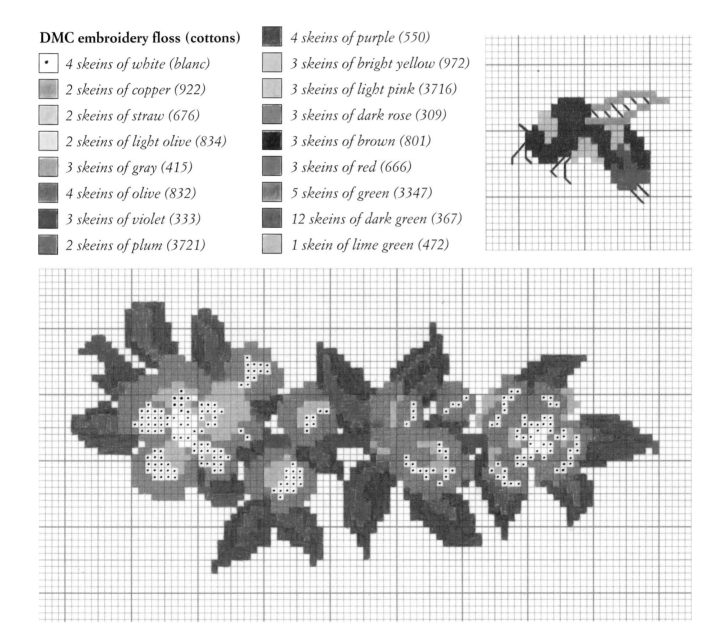

DMC embroidery floss (cottons)

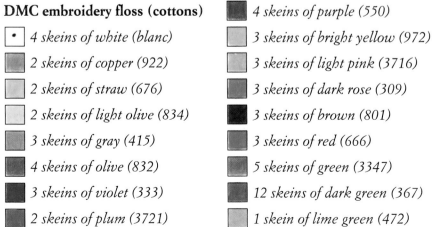

• 4 skeins of white (blanc)	4 skeins of purple (550)
2 skeins of copper (922)	3 skeins of bright yellow (972)
2 skeins of straw (676)	3 skeins of light pink (3716)
2 skeins of light olive (834)	3 skeins of dark rose (309)
3 skeins of gray (415)	3 skeins of brown (801)
4 skeins of olive (832)	3 skeins of red (666)
3 skeins of violet (333)	5 skeins of green (3347)
2 skeins of plum (3721)	12 skeins of dark green (367)
	1 skein of lime green (472)

DMC embroidery floss (cottons)

- • *4 skeins of white (blanc)*
- *2 skeins of copper (922)*
- *2 skeins of straw (676)*
- *2 skeins of light olive (834)*
- *3 skeins of gray (415)*
- *4 skeins of olive (832)*
- *3 skeins of violet (333)*
- *2 skeins of plum (3721)*

- *4 skeins of purple (550)*
- *3 skeins of bright yellow (972)*
- *3 skeins of light pink (3716)*
- *3 skeins of dark rose (309)*
- *3 skeins of brown (801)*
- *3 skeins of red (666)*
- *5 skeins of green (3347)*
- *12 skeins of dark green (367)*
- *1 skein of lime green (472)*

Toadstool Book Cover

I've put these toadstools in this chapter because it is in an orchard that you are most likely to find them. This idea can be adapted to fit any size of book or photo album, and if you want to make it extra special, you could also work the title in cross-stitch.

Actual design measures:
$3\frac{1}{2} \times 3\frac{1}{8}$ in (8.9 × 8 cm)

Materials

1 piece of 28-count Zweigart Linda
   in cream measuring $5\frac{1}{2}$ in
   (14 cm) square
No. 24 tapestry needle
1 piece of cotton fabric long enough
   to go from one end of the book
   to the other plus 7 in (17.8 cm),
   and wide enough to go from top
   to bottom of the book plus
   1 in (2.5 cm)
1 piece of acid-free cardboard
   measuring $4\frac{1}{2}$ in (11.4 cm)
   square
Rubber cement (glue)
3 40-in (101.6-cm) lengths of green
   knitting worsted weight (DK)
   yarn
2 sheets of paper the same size as
   the book cover
1 book

DMC embroidery floss (cottons)

1 skein of red (666)

1 skein of white (blanc)

1 skein of green (906)

1 skein of straw (676)

1 skein of dark olive (830)

1 skein of green (3346)

1 skein of brown (433)

Instructions

Mark the center of the chart and the center of the fabric. Starting here, work in cross-stitch using two threads of floss (cotton) over two strands of fabric. Wrap the cotton fabric around your closed book, folding the raw edges of fabric to the inside of the front and back book covers. Snip the fabric each side of the book's spine at the top and bottom. Fold and glue the top, bottom, front, and back edges of the fabric to the inside of the book covers. Glue and tuck the fabric into the book's spine. Mount the embroidery on the piece of cardboard by stretching the fabric over the card and gluing the edges to the wrong side. Center the mounted work on the front of the book cover and glue in position. Take the two sheets of paper and glue them over the raw edges of the fabric on the inside of the covers to finish them neatly. Twist the lengths of yarn into a rope (see Techniques on page 165). Glue the twisted cord around the embroidered panel, pushing the knotted ends out of sight underneath the cord.

Apples and Bees

This apple and bee design is stitched on a damask dishtowel. You can sometimes find damask items at yard sales, auctions, or in secondhand stores. You can also buy them new (see Suppliers on page 166).

Actual design measures:
9 × 7½ in (22.8 × 19 cm)

Materials
1 piece of 14-count waste canvas measuring 10 in (25.4 cm) square
No. 8 crewel needle
1 damask dishtowel – see Suppliers on page 166
Sewing thread for basting
Sewing needle
Pair of tweezers

DMC embroidery floss (cottons)

- 1 skein of dark rose (309)
- 1 skein of white (blanc)
- 1 skein of pink (3716)
- 1 skein of straw (676)
- 1 skein of yellow (972)
- 1 skein of light olive (834)
- 1 skein of brown (801)
- 1 skein of dark green (367)
- 1 skein of light green (368)
- 1 skein of red (666)
- 1 skein of gray (317)
- 1 skein of dark olive (830)

Instructions

Position the waste canvas at the bottom center of the towel and baste it in place. Mark the center of the canvas and the center of the chart. Starting here, work in cross-stitch using two strands of floss (cotton) until the design is complete. Carefully remove the basting stitches, then pull the strands of waste canvas from under the embroidery with the tweezers.

Blackberry Bag

This is the twin for the Rowan Bag (see page 94). You could wear it tied to a belt at your waist.

Actual design measures: approximately 4 in (10 cm) square

Materials

1 piece of 14-count Zweigart Rustico measuring 7 in (17.8 cm) square
No. 22 tapestry needle
1 piece of printed cotton measuring 32 × 12 in (81.3 × 30.5 cm)
Sewing machine
Sewing thread to match the printed cotton
Sewing needle
2¼ yards (2 meters) of fine cord or twisted yarn

DMC embroidery floss (cottons)

1 skein of purple (550)
1 skein of violet (552)
1 skein of green (367)
1 skein of light green (368)
1 skein of plum (3721)
1 skein of gray (3743)
1 skein of yellow (725)
1 skein of brown (839)
1 skein of gold (729)

Instructions

Mark the center of the chart and the center of the Rustico. Starting here, work in cross-stitch using three strands of floss (cotton). Machine-stitch a hem 2 in (5 cm) deep along each narrow edge of the printed cotton. Fold the fabric in half, wrong sides together. With hems at the top, center the embroidery on the front of the fabric. Turn in the edges of the Rustico to form a 6¼ in (15.9 cm) square and stitch this panel in position. Add a cord border, if you wish. Turn the fabric around so the right sides are together, and machine-stitch up the side seams, with a 1 in (2.5 cm) seam allowance, but do not stitch over the hems. Turn the bag right side out. Cut remaining cord in half. Thread each cord through both hems, knotting ends on the opposite sides of the bag.

Rowan Bag

You could use this bag for storing your seed packs. Hung up next to the Blackberry Bag, it will brighten any room.

Actual design measures:
4¼ × 4 in (10.8 × 10 cm)

Materials
1 piece of 14-count Zweigart
* Rustico measuring 7 in*
* (17.8 cm) square*
No. 22 tapestry needle
1 piece of printed cotton measuring
* 32 × 12 in (81.3 × 30.5 cm)*
Sewing machine
Sewing thread to match the printed
* cotton*
Sewing needle
2¼ yards (2 meters) of fine cord or
* twisted yarn*

DMC embroidery floss (cottons)

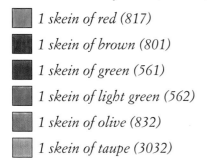

1 skein of red (817)
1 skein of brown (801)
1 skein of green (561)
1 skein of light green (562)
1 skein of olive (832)
1 skein of taupe (3032)

Instructions

Mark the center of the chart and the center of the Rustico. Starting here, work in cross-stitch using three strands of floss (cotton). Machine-stitch a hem 2 in (5 cm) deep along each narrow edge of the printed cotton. Fold the fabric in half, wrong sides together. With hems at the top, center the embroidery on the front of the fabric. Turn in the edges of the Rustico to form a 6¼ in (15.9 cm) square and stitch this panel in position. Add a cord border. Turn the fabric so the right sides are together and stitch up the side seams, with a 1 in (2.5 cm) seam allowance, but do not stitch over the hems. Turn the bag right side out. Topstitch side edges. Cut remaining cord in half. Thread cord or twisted yarn through both hems, knotting ends on the opposite sides of the bag.

Cherry Hat

The instructions for this project explain how to make the complete hat. You could, of course, simply work the motif and stitch it on an existing hat to form a badge, or you could cut out a piece the same size as your brim, work the cross stitch, and then stitch it over the existing brim.

Actual design measures:
2½ × 4¾ in (6.4 × 12 cm)

Materials
*1 piece of 16-count Aida (for brim)
  in sage measuring 19 × 28 in
  (48.2 × 71.1 cm)
No. 24 tapestry needle
1 piece of muslin (calico) (for lining
  the band and crown) measuring
  17 × 30 in (43.2 × 76.2 cm)
1 piece of cotton ticking
  (for the brim, band, and crown)
  measuring 24 × 30 in
  (61 × 76.2 cm)
Tracing paper
Pencil
Sewing machine
Sewing thread
Sewing needle*

DMC embroidery floss (cottons)
*1 skein of red (666)
1 skein of purple (550)
1 skein of straw (676)
1 skein of burgundy (3721)
1 skein of green (367)
1 skein of light green (3347)
1 skein of brown (632)*

Instructions

Enlarge the patterns for the hat (1 square equals 1 cm; 10 cm equals about 4 in). Fold fabric pieces in half and place arrows along fold to cut out. Mark the center of the Aida brim and the center of the chart. Starting here, work in cross-stitch using two strands of floss (cotton) until the design is complete.

With right sides together, stitch the Aida brim to the ticking brim along the curve. Seam the ends of the brim. Turn right side out and baste the brim to the ticking band and stitch it; join the short ends of the band. With the hat inside out, baste and stitch the ticking crown to the band. To line the hat, stitch the lining band to the lining crown. Join the side seam. Wrong sides together, place the lining in the hat. Turn in raw edges and hand-sew the bottom edge of the lining band to the inner edge of the brim.

Enlarge the patterns below for the hat brim, band and crown. One square equals 1 cm.

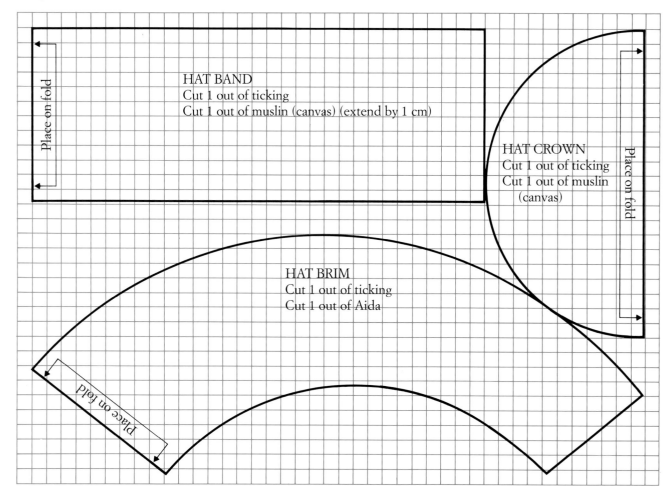

Place on fold

HAT BAND
Cut 1 out of ticking
Cut 1 out of muslin (canvas) (extend by 1 cm)

HAT CROWN
Cut 1 out of ticking
Cut 1 out of muslin
(canvas)

Place on fold

HAT BRIM
Cut 1 out of ticking
Cut 1 out of Aida

Place on fold

Strawberry Tablecloth

Set a summer table with this beautiful cutwork cloth embroidered with strawberries. If you have matching napkins, stitch an individual strawberry in one corner of each.

Central panel measures:
3½ in (8.9 cm) in diameter
Small motifs measure:
1½ in (3.8 cm) square

Materials
1 piece of 14-count waste canvas
measuring 5 in (12.7 cm) square
4 pieces of 14-count waste canvas
measuring 2½ in (6.3 cm) square
No. 8 crewel needle
1 circular cloth trimmed with
Battenberg (tape) lace – see
Suppliers on page 166
Sewing needle
Sewing thread for basting
Pair of tweezers

Instructions
Baste the larger piece of waste canvas to the center of the cloth and the four smaller pieces evenly around the body of the cloth. Mark the center of the central chart and the center of the canvas. Starting here, work in cross-stitch using two strands of floss (cotton). Repeat for the smaller motifs. When the designs are complete, carefully remove the basting stitches, then pull strands of waste canvas from under the embroidery with tweezers.

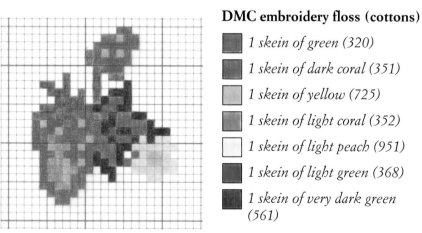

DMC embroidery floss (cottons)

- 1 skein of green (320)
- 1 skein of dark coral (351)
- 1 skein of yellow (725)
- 1 skein of light coral (352)
- 1 skein of light peach (951)
- 1 skein of light green (368)
- 1 skein of very dark green (561)

THE VEGETABLE GARDEN

There is nothing more appetizing than seeing a basket full of freshly-picked carrots and bright green beans. The flowers, shapes, and textures of vegetables make designing with them a delight, particularly when you know that, when you've finished, you can eat them. In my country garden, the vegetables that survive the rabbits are eaten by the slugs. I therefore dedicate this chapter to those wonderfully clever people who grow unblemished prize vegetables. May they continue to give me hope.

Vegetable
Message Board

Zucchini (marrows) and gourds
are perfect subjects for designers.
I have cross-stitched these
zucchini onto a wonderful
evenweave fabric that resembles
burlap (hessian) in both color and
texture. The finished design could
be used in a number of ways, but
I have chosen to mount it on a
message board which will hang in
my greenhouse.

Actual design measures:
$2^{7}/_{8} \times 8$ in $(7.3 \times 20.3$ cm)

Materials
*1 piece of 14-count Zweigart
    Rustico measuring 8 × 11½ in
    (20.3 × 29.2 cm)*
No. 22 tapestry needle
*1 piece of acid-free cardboard
    measuring 6 × 9½ in
    (15.2 × 24.1 cm)*
*1 piece of synthetic batting
    (wadding) measuring 6 × 9½ in
    (15.2 × 24.1 cm)*
*1 piece of board measuring
    approximately 24 × 17 in
    (61 × 43.2 cm)*
*1 piece of orange burlap (hessian)
    measuring 28 × 21 in
    (71.1 × 53.3 cm)*
*14 yards (12.8 meters) of ½ in
    (12 mm) wide green ribbon*
Rubber cement (glue)

DMC embroidery floss (cottons)

- 1 *skein of green (3346)*
- 1 *skein of yellow (743)*
- 1 *skein of cream (3047)*
- 1 *skein of light green (471)*
- 1 *skein of dark green (561)*
- 1 *skein of orange (741)*
- 1 *skein of light orange (977)*
- 1 *skein of copper (720)*
- 1 *skein of light olive (834)*

Instructions

Mark the center of the chart and the center of the Rustico. Starting here, work the design in cross-stitch using three strands of floss (cotton). Where backstitch is indicated, use two strands of floss (cotton). Glue the batting (wadding) to the front of the small piece of cardboard. Leave to dry. Stretch the design over the covered cardboard, centering the design carefully, and glue the raw edges to the back.

Cover the large board with the burlap (hessian). Cut two lengths of ribbon, each measuring 32 in (81.3 cm), and glue them from the top corners to the opposite bottom corners of the board to form a cross. Starting from the top edge, attach more ribbons so they run parallel to the first ribbons and are spaced about 2 in (5 cm) apart. Glue the ends to the back. Now continue the process, covering the board and weaving the ribbons in and out of those already in place. When the trellis of ribbons is complete, glue the cross-stitched panel in the center of the top of the board. Glue a loop of ribbon to the back of the board, centered at the top edge, so you can hang up the message board.

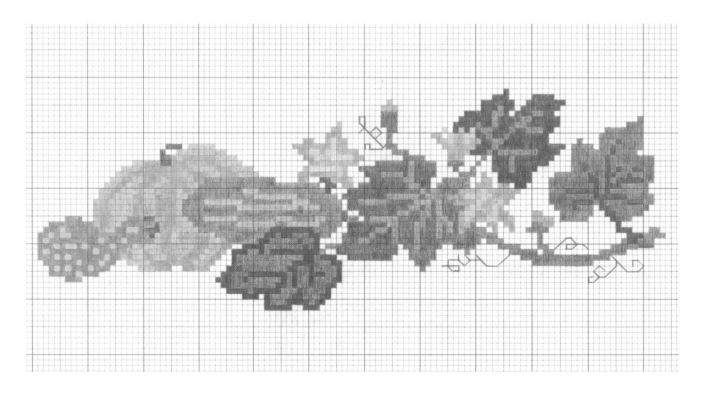

Bag of Bunnies

You can buy some very unusual fabrics designed for cross-stitch, and this oatmeal-colored Aida is no exception. I have made a simple bag from orange burlap (hessian) and stitched the cross-stitch sampler to the front of it. If you don't want to make a bag, you could frame the sampler and hang it in your kitchen.

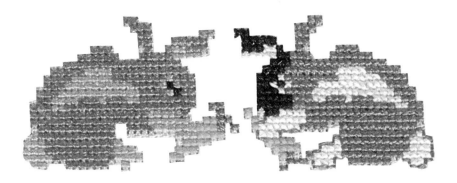

DMC embroidery floss (cottons)

- 1 skein of black (310)
- 1 skein of orange (740)
- 1 skein of khaki (830)
- 1 skein of old gold (729)
- 1 skein of dark green (469)
- 1 skein of white (blanc)
- 1 skein of light gray (3743)
- 1 skein of dark gray (451)
- 1 skein of light green (3348)
- 1 skein of green (907)
- 1 skein of red (606)

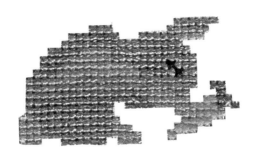

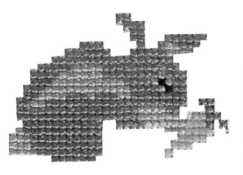

Actual design measures:
14 × 12 in (35.5 × 30 cm)

Materials

1 piece of 14-count Aida in oatmeal
measuring 18 × 16 in
(45.7 × 40.6 cm)
No. 22 tapestry needle
2 pieces of orange burlap (hessian),
each measuring 22 × 27 in
(55.9 × 68.6 cm)
1 piece of orange burlap (hessian)
measuring 6 × 40 in
(15.2 × 101.6 cm)
Pins
Sewing thread for basting
Sewing threads to match Aida and
burlap (hessian)
Sewing machine

Instructions

Mark the center of the chart and
the center of the Aida. Starting
here, work in cross-stitch using

three strands of floss (cotton).
Stitch the outlines of the rabbits
(white areas only) in backstitch
using two strands of old gold.
When the design is complete, turn
under the raw edges of the Aida
and pin to the middle of one of the
large pieces of burlap (hessian),
leaving 3½ in (8.9 cm) at the
bottom, and 5 in (12.7 cm) at the
top. Turn back and baste a ½ in
(12 mm) hem of burlap at each
side and 1½ in (3.8 cm) at the top.

Machine-stitch along the top of the
burlap, then remove the basting
stitches. Hem the second piece of
burlap the same way as the first.
Place the front on the back of the
bag with wrong sides together and
machine-stitch along the sides and
bottom to form a bag. To make the
handle, fold the remaining strip of
burlap in half lengthwise and
machine-stitch the seam. Turn the
handle inside out and topstitch
½ in (12 mm) in from each side.
Stitch the short ends securely to
the inside of the bag across the
side seams.

Bunny
Thermometer

Why not decorate a thermometer to hang in your greenhouse? You can buy thermometers and barometers by mail (see Suppliers on page 166). For mine, I've used some bunnies who have escaped from the vegetable patch, but you could adapt many of the designs in this book instead.

Actual design measures:
10¼ × 4¼ in (26 × 10.8 cm)

Materials
1 piece of 14-count Aida in cream
*   measuring 13¼ × 7¼ in*
*   (33.6 × 18.4 cm)*
No. 22 tapestry needle
1 piece of acid-free cardboard
*   measuring 11 × 5 in*
*   (28 × 12.7 cm)*
1 mounted thermometer,
*   measuring 7 × 1¼ in*
*   (17.8 × 3.2 cm)*
Brass loop or self-adhesive picture
*   hook*
Rubber cement (glue)

DMC embroidery floss (cottons)

- ■ *1 skein of brown (801)*
- ■ *1 skein of dark green (469)*
- · *1 skein of white (blanc)*
- ▨ *1 skein of old gold (729)*
- ■ *1 skein of black (310)*
- ▨ *1 skein of red (606)*
- ▨ *1 skein of light green (3348)*
- ▨ *1 skein of dark gray (451)*
- ▨ *1 skein of light gray (3743)*
- ▨ *1 skein of orange (740)*
- ╲ *Backstitch in old gold (729)*

Instructions

Mark the center of your chart and the center of the Aida. Starting here, work the design in cross-stitch using three strands of floss (cotton). Stitch the outline of the rabbits (white areas only) in backstitch using two strands of old gold. When the design is complete, stretch it over the cardboard and glue the raw edges of Aida to the back. Glue the mounted thermometer to the center front, and attach the brass loop or picture hook to the center top of the back of the board.

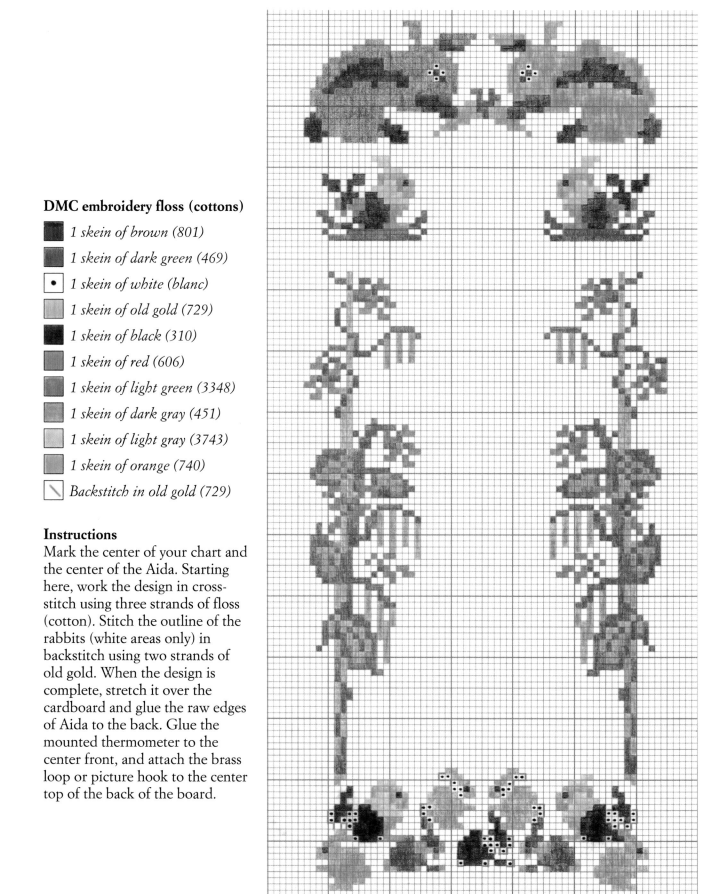

Mushrooms and Cheese

I have used this mushroom design to decorate an empty cheese box that originally contained camembert. For goodness sake, wash any food boxes with bleach before you decorate them with cross-stitch; otherwise, you'll end up with something very smelly – or worse.

Actual design measures:
3³⁄₄ × 3¹⁄₄ in (9.5 × 8.3 cm)

Materials

1 piece of 28-count Zweigart Linda in pink measuring 1 in (2.5 cm) larger in diameter than the center of the box lid
No. 24 tapestry needle
Camembert cheese box and lid
1 piece of acid-free cardboard, the exact diameter of the box lid
1 piece of synthetic batting (wadding) the exact diameter of the box lid
Rubber cement (glue)

DMC embroidery floss (cottons)

	1 skein of yellow (744)
	1 skein of silver beige (3033)
	1 skein of mustard (729)
	1 skein of khaki (830)
	1 skein of ecru (746)
	1 skein of green (934)
	1 skein of brown (839)
	1 skein of gray (535)
	Straight stitch in gray (535)

Instructions

Mark the center of the chart and the center of the fabric. Starting here, work in cross-stitch using two strands of floss (cotton) over two threads of fabric. Work the straight stitch detail (on leaves) using one strand of floss. Glue the batting (wadding) to the top of the cardboard and leave to dry. Stretch the completed cross-stitch design over the cardboard, centering it, and glue the raw edges to the underside, clipping edges. Leave to dry. Glue this padded panel to the top of the box lid.

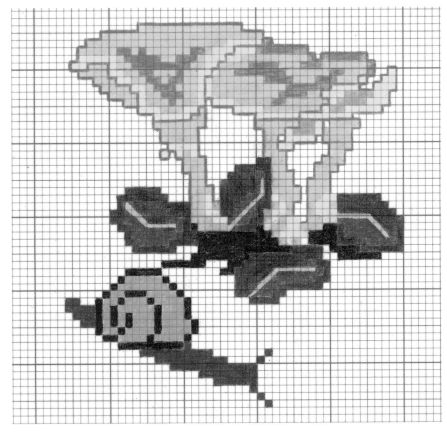

Brown Mushrooms

I love decorating boxes. To keep the natural character of the wood, I've used burlap (hessian) and twisted "rope" made from some camel-colored knitting yarn. There are various mushroom designs in this book, all of a similar size. You could group them together in one big sampler or use them to make a patchwork coverlet incorporating pretty fabrics in harmonizing colors.

Actual design measures:
3¼ × 3 in (8.3 × 7.6 cm)

Materials

1 piece of 28-count Zweigart Linda in rose measuring 7 × 6 in (17.8 × 15.2 cm)
No. 24 tapestry needle
1 piece of acid-free cardboard measuring 4¾ × 7½ in (12 × 19 cm) or to fit the top of the box
1 wooden box
1 piece of synthetic batting (wadding) measuring 4¾ × 7½ in (12 × 19 cm) or to fit the top of the box
1 piece of natural burlap (hessian) measuring 6½ × 10 in (16.5 × 25.4 cm) or to fit the top of the box plus 1 in (2.5 cm) all around
18 yards (16 meters) knitting worsted weight (DK) yarn in camel
Rubber cement (glue)
Sewing thread to match the Linda
Sewing needle

Instructions

Mark the center of your chart and the center of the fabric. Starting here, work the design in cross-stitch using two strands of floss (cotton) and working over two threads of fabric. When the design is complete, fold under the raw edges of the fabric and stitch it to the center of the piece of burlap (hessian). Glue the batting (wadding) to the top of the cardboard. Leave to dry. Stretch the burlap over the cardboard, centering the design; then glue the

raw edges to the back of the cardboard. Glue this padded panel to the center of the box lid. Make a cord by folding a 7-yard (6.4-meter) length of the knitting yarn in three and twisting it (see Techniques on page 165). Glue this "rope" carefully around the piece of cross-stitch. Make a thicker cord by folding the remaining yarn in five and twisting it. Glue this cord around the edge of the mounted work.

DMC embroidery floss (cottons)

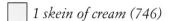 *1 skein of silver beige (3033)*   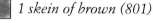 *1 skein of brown (801)*

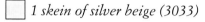 *1 skein of cream (746)*   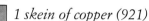 *1 skein of copper (921)*

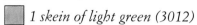 *1 skein of light green (3012)*   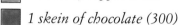 *1 skein of chocolate (300)*

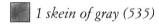 *1 skein of gray (535)*   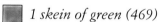 *1 skein of green (469)*

Mushroom Pillbox

These little mushrooms could be repeated to make a border for a sampler, or you could mount just one small motif on the top of a Framecraft box (see Suppliers on page 166). If you work the design on a larger-count fabric you could make a bag to keep dried mushrooms in.

Actual design measures:
1 in (2.5 cm) square

Materials

1 piece of 32-count linen in ecru measuring 4 in (10 cm) square
No. 24 tapestry needle
1 Framecraft pillbox – see Suppliers on page 166

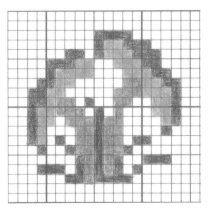

DMC embroidery floss (cottons)

1 skein of mushroom (3042)

1 skein of yellow (742)

1 skein of green (469)

1 skein of dark mushroom (3041)

Instructions

Mark the center of the chart and the center of the fabric. Starting here, work the design in cross-stitch using two strands of floss (cotton). Mount completed design in lid of pillbox.

Sweet Pea

Frame your own sweet pea in this little photo frame. If you happen to be your favorite person, you could frame a mirror instead, or you could use the design as a diary cover and embroider the year in the center of the front cover.

Actual design measures:
5 × 4¼ in (12.7 × 11.4 cm)

Materials

1 piece of 28-count Zweigart Linda in ivory measuring 10½ in (26.6 cm) square
No. 24 tapestry needle
2 pieces of acid-free cardboard, each measuring 8¼ × 7½ in (21 × 19 cm)
1 piece of synthetic batting (wadding) measuring 8¼ × 7½ in (21 × 19 cm)
Rubber cement (glue)
Craft knife
Self-adhesive picture hook

DMC embroidery floss (cottons)

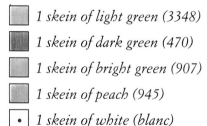

1 skein of light green (3348)
1 skein of dark green (470)
1 skein of bright green (907)
1 skein of peach (945)
1 skein of white (blanc)

Instructions

Mark the center of the chart and the center of the fabric. Starting here, work the design in cross-stitch using two strands of floss (cotton). Where backstitch is indicated, use one strand of light green. Glue the batting (wadding) to one piece of cardboard and leave to dry. With the craft knife, cut out an area in the center of this cardboard to fit your photograph. Stretch the finished cross-stitch over the piece of padded cardboard; glue the raw edges to the back. Make cuts from the center of the fabric to each inside corner of the cardboard. Fold the fabric to the back of the cardboard, then stretch, trim the excess, and glue in place.

On the remaining cardboard, dab glue around the bottom edge and along the two sides. Glue this to the back of your design. Leave to dry. Slide your photograph in through the top. Attach a self-adhesive hook to the back.

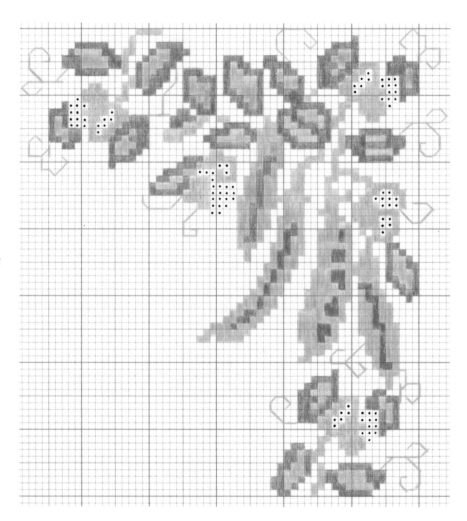

THE
WATER GARDEN

The water garden is home to all manner of winged and waterbound creatures. My own pond, dug simply to drain a soggy meadow, has been a source of great pleasure to me. Within a month of completing it, I had many new neighbors; damselflies, herons, and newts splashed around in their new home. The following projects are based on my new friends. I have suggested a few ideas, but I'm sure you will have many more. You can repeat the smaller motifs to form a border or picture frame.

Heron and Lilies Folder

One morning, I noticed a heron standing one-legged on the roof of a house in the center of London. He was beadily looking at a tiny pond (more of a puddle, really) in the backyard below. There he stood like a stone statue until, in the blink of an eye, he swooped – and it was goldfish for breakfast.

Actual design measures:
6½ × 7½ in (16.5 × 19 cm)

Materials

1 piece of 28-count Zweigart Linda
  in rose measuring 14 in
  (35.5 cm) square
No. 24 tapestry needle
3 pieces of satin fabric in aqua,
  each measuring 14 in (35.5 cm)
  square
1 piece of satin fabric in aqua
  measuring 13 × 3 in
  (33 × 7.6 cm)
1 piece of synthetic batting
  (wadding) measuring
  10 × 11 in (25.4 × 28 cm)
2 pieces of heavy acid-free
  cardboard, each measuring
  10 × 11 in (25.4 × 28 cm)
2 pieces of thin acid-free cardboard,
  each measuring 9³/4 × 10³/4 in
  (24.7 × 27.3 cm)
Rubber cement (glue)
18 in (45.7 cm) of narrow ribbon
1 wooden bead

DMC embroidery floss (cottons)

- 1 skein of white (blanc)
- 1 skein of yellow (744)
- 1 skein of copper (922)
- 1 skein of black (310)
- 1 skein of gray (451)
- 1 skein of dark gray (535)

- 1 skein of light green (471)
- 1 skein of light peach (951)
- 1 skein of green (3346)
- 1 skein of dark green (936)
- 1 skein of pale green (966)

Instructions

Mark the center of the chart and the center of the fabric. Starting here, use two strands of floss (cotton) over two threads of fabric. Work from here in cross-stitch until the design is complete. Glue the batting (wadding) to the front of one piece of heavy cardboard and leave to dry. Stretch the finished design over

the batting, centering it carefully, and glue the raw edges to the back. This is your front piece. Set it aside.

Cover the other piece of heavy cardboard with one of the square pieces of aqua satin, leaving 2 in (5 cm) of fabric free at the left edge for the spine. This is for the back of the folder. Cover the two pieces of thin cardboard with the other pieces of square aqua satin and glue the raw edges to the back. These are the two inside panels.

Lay the front and back pieces side by side, face down. Join them together by gluing 1 in (2.5 cm) of the fabric intended for the spine to the adjoining edge of the front of the folder. Take the small piece of aqua satin and glue it to the spine, folding in and gluing the top and bottom edges to give a neat finish. Finally, glue the two inside panels to the front and back of the folder to hide all the raw edges. Leave to dry. Glue one end of the ribbon to the center top of the spine, thread the wooden bead through the other end of the ribbon, and knot the ribbon to make a bookmark.

Grasshopper Box

Small motifs can be worked in no time at all and, when mounted attractively, make lovely gifts. I think these little Framecraft boxes are charming, and when you use your first one it could herald the beginning of a magnificent collection. The boxes are available in lots of different colors and various shapes (see Suppliers on page 166).

Actual design measures:
1⅛ in (2.9 cm) square

Materials

1 piece of 32-count natural linen measuring 4 in (10 cm) square
No. 24 tapestry needle
1 Framecraft box – see Suppliers on page 166

Instructions

Mark the center of the chart and the center of the fabric. Starting here, use two strands of floss (cotton) except when working in green, when you should use one strand of floss and one strand of Blending Filament. Work in cross-stitch over two threads of fabric until the design is complete. Mount according to the manufacturer's directions.

DMC embroidery floss (cottons)

1 skein of green (906) plus 1 spool of Kreinik Metallics Blending Filament 015

1 skein of mustard (729)

1 skein of black (310)

1 skein of red (666)

1 skein of yellow (742)

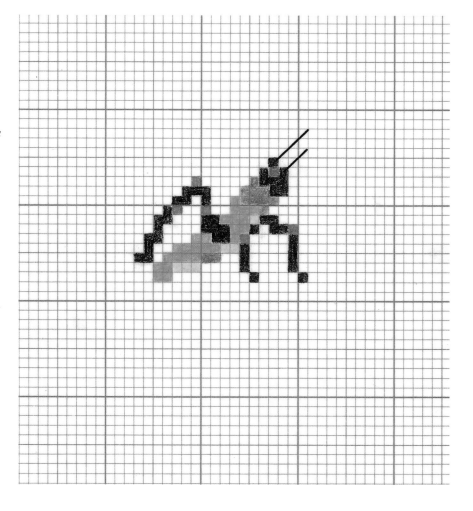

Damselfly Box

This pretty winged creature, along with the dragonfly, graces the pond with her silvery wings. Stitch her on a box lid or add her to a sampler based on all your favorite backyard friends.

Actual design measures:
1⅛ in (2.9 cm) square

Materials
1 piece of 32-count natural linen measuring 4 in (10 cm) square
No. 24 tapestry needle
1 Framecraft box – see Suppliers on page 166

DMC embroidery floss (cottons)

1 skein of red (326)

1 skein of green (469)

1 skein of mushroom (3042) plus 1 spool of Kreinik Metallics Blending Filament 025

1 skein of black (310) plus 1 spool of Kreinik Metallics Blending Filament 085

1 skein of yellow (742)

Straight stitch in black (310)

Instructions
Mark the center of the chart and the center of the fabric. Starting here, use two strands of floss (cotton) except where mushroom and black are indicated, when you should use one strand of floss and one strand of Blending Filament. Work in cross-stitch over two threads of fabric until the design is complete. Mount according to the manufacturer's directions.

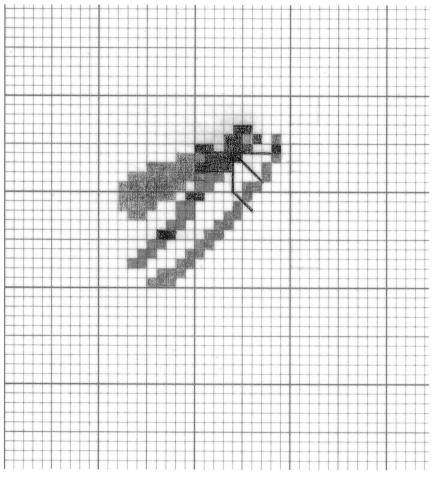

Ladybug Box

The ladybug (ladybird) is the gardener's friend because it feeds on aphids and scale-insect pests. It is also a favorite motif with children and adults alike. I have added to my collection of little boxes with this one and have used her in other projects where she seems at home.

Actual design measures:
⅞ in (2.2 cm) square

Materials

1 piece of 32-count natural linen measuring 4 in (10 cm) square
No. 24 tapestry needle
1 Framecraft box – see Suppliers on page 166

Instructions

Mark the center of the chart and the center of the fabric. Starting here, work in cross-stitch using two strands of floss over two threads of fabric until the design is complete. Mount following the manufacturer's directions.

DMC embroidery floss (cottons)

 1 skein of red (666)

 1 skein of black (310)

 Straight stitch in black (310)

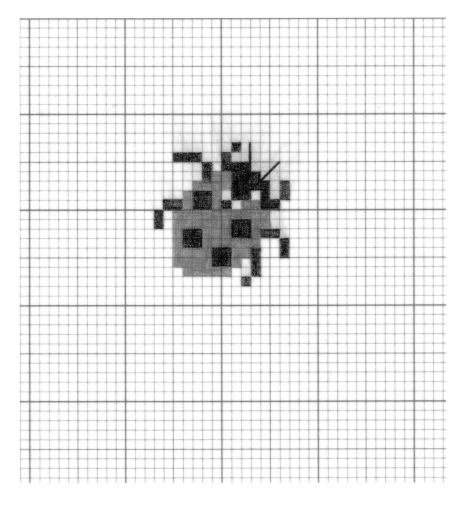

Goldfish Key Holder

Cross-stitch panels can be used to cover all sorts of items, and this little key holder is a good example. Mount your finished work on a board and glue the board to the front panel.
You could treat door panels in the same way. Or, you could cross-stitch the door of your bedroom closet. Now that's something to think about …

Actual design measures:
5³⁄₄ × 3¹⁄₂ in (14.7 × 8.8 cm)

Materials

1 piece of 18-count Aida in cream measuring 10 × 8 in (25.4 × 20.3 cm) or 4 in (10 cm) larger all around than the panel
No. 25 tapestry needle
1 small wooden cabinet
1 piece of acid-free cardboard measuring 5³⁄₄ × 3¹⁄₂ in (14.7 × 8.8 cm) or the same size as the panel
Rubber cement (glue)

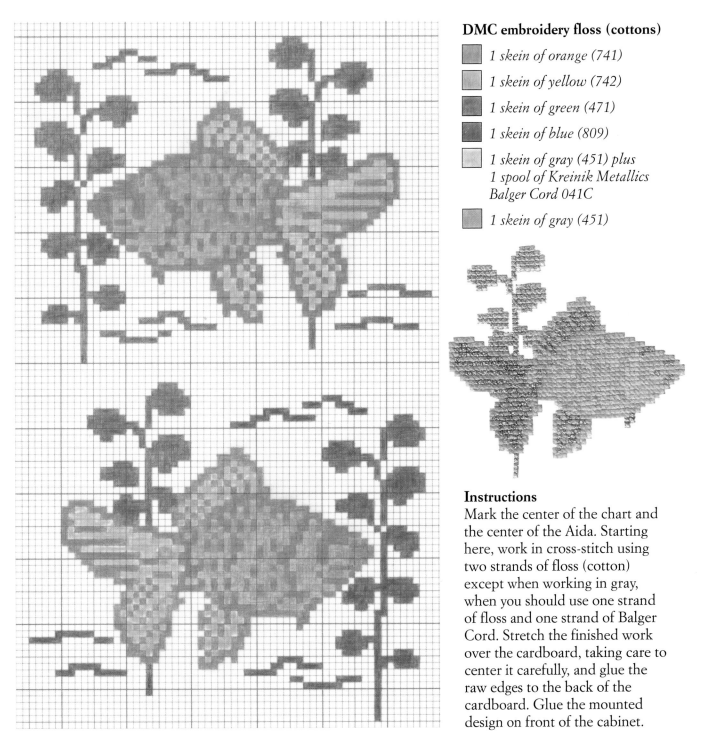

DMC embroidery floss (cottons)

- 1 skein of orange (741)
- 1 skein of yellow (742)
- 1 skein of green (471)
- 1 skein of blue (809)
- 1 skein of gray (451) plus
  1 spool of Kreinik Metallics
  Balger Cord 041C
- 1 skein of gray (451)

Instructions

Mark the center of the chart and the center of the Aida. Starting here, work in cross-stitch using two strands of floss (cotton) except when working in gray, when you should use one strand of floss and one strand of Balger Cord. Stretch the finished work over the cardboard, taking care to center it carefully, and glue the raw edges to the back of the cardboard. Glue the mounted design on front of the cabinet.

Frogs in the Looking Glass

This friendly frog is designed to make you look good, even first thing in the morning. I have stitched him on Linda fabric, but you can use 14-count Aida if you prefer.

Actual design measures:
5¼ × 10¼ in (13.4 × 26 cm)

Materials

1 piece of 28-count Zweigart Linda in pink measuring 14½ × 15½ in (36.8 × 39.4 cm)
No. 24 tapestry needle
2 pieces of medium-weight acid-free cardboard, each measuring 11½ × 12½ in (29.2 × 31.7 cm)
1 piece of synthetic batting (wadding) measuring 11½ × 12½ in (29.2 × 31.7 cm)
Round mirror measuring 5 in (12.7 cm) in diameter
24 in (61 cm) of piping
Rubber cement (glue)
Sewing thread to match the piping
Sewing needle

DMC embroidery floss (cottons)

1 skein of cream (746)
1 skein of black (310)
1 skein of brown-gray (3790)
1 skein of khaki (830)
1 skein of dark rose (3721)
1 skein of yellow (743)
1 skein of light rose (223)
1 skein of green (3346)
1 skein of light green (471)
1 skein of beige (3782)
1 skein of brown (801)

Instructions

Beginning at the bottom left-hand edge of the chart, place the first stitch 2½ in (6.3 cm) up from the bottom of the fabric and 2 in (5 cm) in from the left-hand edge. Work in cross-stitch using two strands of floss (cotton) over two threads of fabric until the design is complete. Finish off neatly.

Glue the batting (wadding) on top of one piece of cardboard. Stretch the finished design over the top, taking care to center it, and glue the raw edges to the back of the cardboard. Cut a small length of cord to form a loop, and glue to the center of the top edge of the back of the cardboard. Glue the second piece of cardboard to the back of the work, with the loop hanging free. Glue the mirror to the front of the work, 1 in (2.5 cm) from the top left-hand edge. Glue the piping neatly around the mirror, stitching the ends together if necessary.

Fountain

The cupid that I have used as inspiration for this design actually stands in my bathroom handing out toilet tissues. He would look much more at home in a formal garden under a halo of crystal-clear droplets of water. Let's hope that this design will restore any dignity that his current role in my house denies him. I have used Kreinik Metallics threads in this design – they really do add a new dimension to cross-stitch.

Actual design measures:
7 in (17.8 cm) square

Materials
1 piece of 14-count Aida in peach, measuring 11 in (28 cm) square
No. 22 tapestry needle
Your choice of frame

DMC embroidery floss (cottons)

- 1 skein of light gray (762)
- 1 skein of green (469)
- 1 skein of violet (553)
- 1 skein of blue (793)
- 1 skein of pink (956)
- 1 skein of yellow (742)
- 1 skein of red (606)
- 1 skein of light green (471)
- 1 skein of white (blanc)
- 1 skein of aqua (564) plus 1 spool of Kreinik Metallics Blending Filament 044
- 1 skein of dark gray (414)
- 1 spool of Kreinik Metallics Blending Filament 041
- 1 skein of dark green (367)

Instructions

Mark the center of the chart and the center of the canvas. Starting here, use three strands of floss (cotton) except where aqua is indicated, when you should use one strand of floss and three strands of Blending Filament. Work in cross-stitch, finally adding the water for the fountain using two strands of Blending Filament 041 in straight stitch. Frame as you wish.

THE WILDLIFE
GARDEN

Embroiderers have always found animals and birds inspiring because they can be interpreted in so many different styles. This chapter includes a simple bluebird motif on a cutwork napkin and a squirrel hoarding his autumn harvest on the pocket of a gardening apron. Stitch pictures of your favorite creatures and hang them on the wall, or cover tin cans with your finished work and use them to store your seed markers and pencils. I hope you enjoy making these projects.

Bluebirds

These bluebird sweethearts are stitched on one half of a napkin edged with Battenberg (tape) lace. I then folded the napkin in two, joined two edges, and inserted a pad of rolled-up batting (wadding) before stitching up the third edge. You could add an herb bag or drop some perfumed oil onto the batting to turn this into an aromatic pillow which will help you sleep.

Actual design measures:
5⅛ in (13 cm) square

Materials
1 piece of 14-count Aida in white
measuring 8 in (20.3 cm) square
No. 22 tapestry needle
1 napkin trimmed with Battenberg
(tape) lace measuring 14 in
(35.5 cm) square
1 piece of batting (wadding)
measuring 28 × 7 in
(71.1 × 17.8 cm)
1 yard (0.9 meter) of narrow blue
satin ribbon
4 small ribbon bows
Sewing thread to match the Aida
Sewing needle
Rubber cement (glue), or sewing
thread to match the ribbon

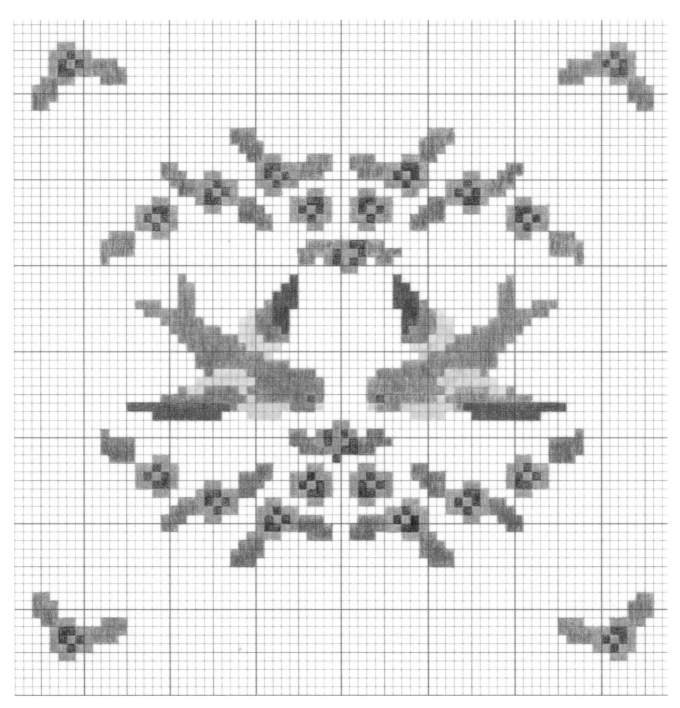

DMC embroidery floss (cottons)

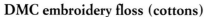 *1 skein of blue (793)*

1 skein of dark blue (792)

1 skein of pale blue (3325)

1 skein of plum (3721)

1 skein of bright pink (893)

1 skein of green (3347)

1 skein of yellow (725)

Instructions

Mark the center of the chart and the center of the Aida. Starting here, work in cross-stitch using three strands of floss (cotton) until the design is complete. Fold the napkin in half and place the Aida panel in the center of one half. Fold back the raw edges of the panel and carefully stitch it in position on the napkin. Sew or glue the ribbon around the edges of the panel, and then stitch or glue one bow to each of the four corners. Sew two sides of the napkin together. Roll the batting (wadding) into shape and insert it in the napkin, then neatly sew up the third side of the napkin.

Blue Tit
Paperweight

This little fellow will make sure that your papers don't fly away whenever you open the window. He is mounted in an oval Framecraft paperweight which you can buy in various shapes (see Suppliers on page 166).

Actual design measures:
$1^{7}/_{8} \times 3$ in (4.7 × 7.6 cm)

Materials
1 piece of 18-count Aida in cream measuring 4 × 6 in (10 × 15.2 cm)
No. 25 tapestry needle
1 oval Framecraft paperweight – see Suppliers on page 166

Instructions
Mark the center of the chart and the center of the Aida. Starting here, work in cross-stitch using three strands of floss (cotton) until the design is complete. Mount the design in the paperweight following the manufacturer's directions.

DMC embroidery floss (cottons)

- ⊡ 1 skein of white (blanc)
- ■ 1 skein of black (310)
- ■ 1 skein of brown (801)
- ■ 1 skein of gray (535)
- ■ 1 skein of green (469)
- ■ 1 skein of turquoise (597)
- ■ 1 skein of light green (471)
- ☐ 1 skein of yellow (307)

Robin Napkin

This red-breasted robin is sitting pretty on a napkin edged with Battenberg (tape) lace. Use him as a motif for a card, or stitch him on Aida and sew him to the front of a muslin (calico) or red gingham bag in which you can store nuts and seeds for the birds.

Actual design measures: about 3 in (7.5 cm) square

Materials

1 piece of 14-count waste canvas measuring 4 in (10 cm) square
No. 8 crewel needle
1 napkin trimmed with Battenberg (tape) lace measuring 14 in (35.5 cm) square
Sewing thread for basting
Sewing needle
Pair of tweezers

DMC embroidery floss (cottons)

- *1 skein of yellow (676)*
- *1 skein of coral (891)*
- *1 skein of black (310)*
- *1 skein of stone (3033)*
- *1 skein of dark olive (830)*
- *1 skein of beige (3032)*
- *1 skein of brown (839)*
- *1 skein of white (blanc)*

Instructions

Baste the waste canvas, diagonally, to the bottom right-hand corner of the napkin. Mark the center of the chart and the center of the waste canvas. Starting here, work in cross-stitch using two strands of floss (cotton). When the design is complete, remove the basting stitches, then pull the strands of waste canvas from under the embroidery with the tweezers.

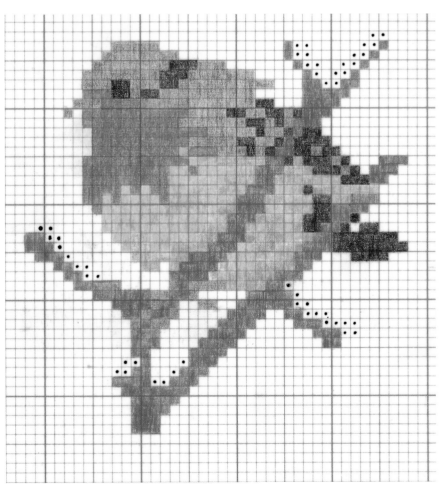

Thrush Napkin

If you have used the robin design for your winter table napkins, here is a companion for the spring. If you are a bird-lover, why not stitch all the birds in this book onto one big sampler.

Actual design measures:
2⅝ × 4¼ in (6.7 × 10.7 cm)

Materials
1 piece of 14-count waste canvas measuring 4 in (10 cm) square
No. 8 crewel needle
1 napkin trimmed with Battenberg (tape) lace measuring 14 in (35.5 cm) square
Sewing thread for basting
Sewing needle
Pair of tweezers

Instructions
Baste the waste canvas to the bottom right-hand corner of the napkin. Mark the center of the chart and the center of the waste canvas. Starting here, work in cross-stitch using two strands of floss (cotton). When the design is complete, carefully remove the basting stitches, then pull the strands of waste canvas from under the embroidery with the tweezers.

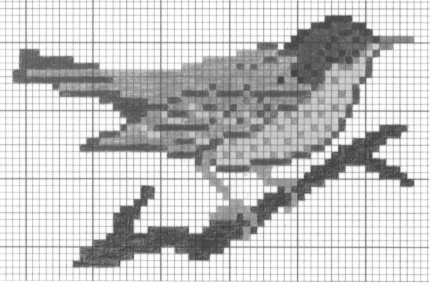

DMC embroidery floss (cottons)

■	*1 skein of beige (3032)*	■	*1 skein of brown (433)*
■	*1 skein of caramel (436)*	□	*1 skein of cream (677)*
■	*1 skein of light orange (977)*	■	*1 skein of orange (720)*
■	*1 skein of stone (453)*		

Barn Owl

Add a painted moon and frame this owl as one of a trio. You can buy precut mat (mounting) boards or cut your own using a carpenter's square and craft knife. Cover with fabric to coordinate with your furnishings. If you do not want to tackle the job yourself, ask your local framer.

Actual design measures: approximately 2¾ × 3½ in (7 × 8.9 cm)

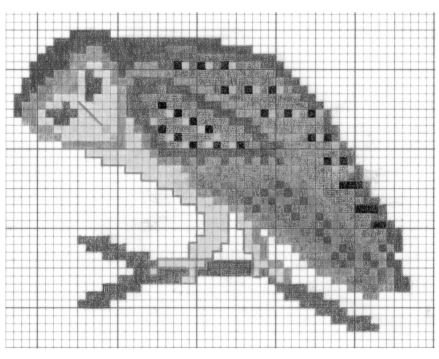

Materials

1 piece of 28-count Zweigart Linda in pale blue measuring 10½ × 13 in (26.6 × 33 cm)

No. 24 tapestry needle

2 pieces of acid-free mat (mounting) board, each measuring 8½ in (21.6 cm) square

1 piece of synthetic batting (wadding) measuring 6 × 8½ in (15.2 × 21.6 cm)

1 piece of burlap (hessian) measuring 11 × 13 in (28 × 33 cm)

Rubber cement (glue)

1 glitter paint pen in silver

1 pencil

DMC Flower Threads

1 skein of dark brown (2839)

1 skein of gray (2773)

1 skein of ecru (ecru)

1 skein of old gold (2782)

1 skein of brown (2609)

1 skein of black (2310)

1 skein of yellow (2748)

Backstitch in gray (2773)

Instructions

Mark the center of the chart and the center of the fabric. Starting here, work in cross-stitch, using two strands of Flower Thread over two threads of fabric, until the design is complete.

Cut out the center square from one piece of mat (mounting) board, leaving a frame that is 1¼ in (3.2 cm) wide. Cut the batting (wadding) into 1¼ in (3.2 cm) strips and glue them into position on the front of the frame. Leave to dry. Carefully position the burlap (hessian) over the padded mat and glue the raw edges to the back of the cardboard. Leaving a border of burlap ¾ in (18 mm) deep, cut away the center square of burlap. Snip the corners diagonally and glue the inner edges of the fabric to the back of the frame.

Mount your design on the remaining piece of board, gluing the raw edges to the back. Leave to dry. Glue the frame to the front of the design and leave to dry. With a pencil, draw in a moon shape at the top right-hand corner of the picture, go over the outline with the silver glitter pen, and then fill in the shape with silver glitter paint.

Horned Owl

This long-eared fellow is another in the owl trio. I think he's rather handsome. He would also look good as a book cover – perhaps for a book on birds.

Actual design measures:
5 × 2 in (12.7 × 5 cm)

Materials
1 piece of 28-count Zweigart Linda in light blue measuring 13¾ × 11¼ in (35 × 28.5 cm)
No. 24 tapestry needle
2 pieces of acid-free mat (mounting) board, each measuring 11¾ × 9¼ in (29.9 × 23.5 cm)
1 piece of synthetic batting (wadding) measuring 11¾ × 6 in (29.9 × 15.2 cm)
1 piece of burlap (hessian) measuring 13 × 11 in (33 × 28 cm)
Rubber cement (glue)
1 glitter paint pen in silver
1 pencil

DMC Flower Threads
1 skein of light brown (2433)
1 skein of rust (2766)
1 skein of brown (2938)
1 skein of ecru (ecru)
1 skein of beige (2436)
1 skein of dark brown (2371)

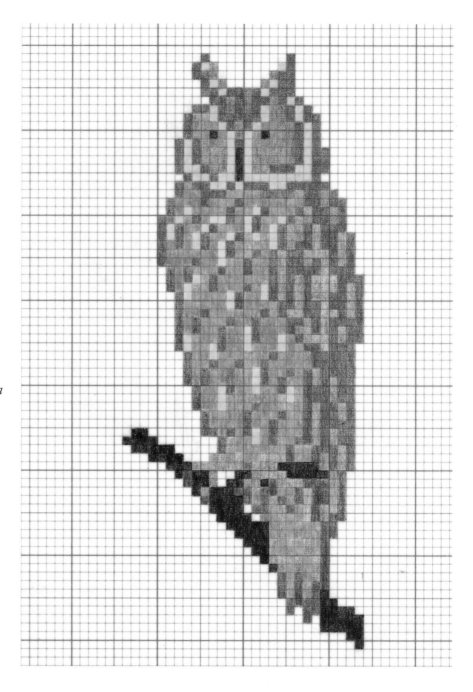

Instructions
Mark the center of the chart and the center of the fabric. Starting here, work in cross-stitch, using two strands of Flower Thread over two threads of fabric, until the design is complete.

Cut out the center square from one piece of mat (mounting) board, leaving a frame that is 1¼ in (3.2 cm) wide. Cut the batting (wadding) into 1¼ in (3.2 cm) strips and glue them in position on the front of the frame. Leave to dry. Carefully position the burlap (hessian) over the padded mat and glue the raw edges to the back of the board. Leaving a border of burlap ¾ in (18 mm) deep, cut away the center square of burlap. Snip the corners diagonally and glue the inner edges of the fabric to the back of the frame.

Mount your design on the remaining piece of board, gluing

Snowy Owl

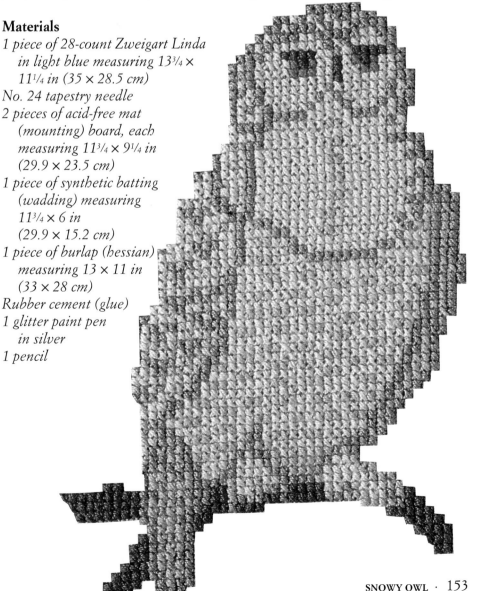

You can frame this third owl or you can mount the Snowy Owl on a board and add some coat hooks. You could also glue him to the top of a box. Either way, he will watchfully guard your possessions.

Actual design measures:
5 × 3¼ in (12.7 × 8.2 cm)

Materials
1 piece of 28-count Zweigart Linda in light blue measuring 13¾ × 11¼ in (35 × 28.5 cm)
No. 24 tapestry needle
2 pieces of acid-free mat (mounting) board, each measuring 11¾ × 9¼ in (29.9 × 23.5 cm)
1 piece of synthetic batting (wadding) measuring 11¾ × 6 in (29.9 × 15.2 cm)
1 piece of burlap (hessian) measuring 13 × 11 in (33 × 28 cm)
Rubber cement (glue)
1 glitter paint pen in silver
1 pencil

Instructions
Mark the center of the chart and the center of the fabric. Starting here, work in cross-stitch, using two strands of Flower Thread over two threads of fabric, until the design is complete.

Cut out the center square from one piece of mat (mounting)

the raw edges to the back. Leave to dry. Glue the frame to the front of the design and leave to dry. With a pencil, draw in a moon shape at the top right-hand corner of the picture, go over the outline with the silver glitter pen, and then fill in the shape with silver glitter paint.

board, leaving a frame that is 1¼ in (3.2 cm) wide. Cut the batting (wadding) into 1¼ in (3.2 cm) strips and glue them in position on the front of the frame. Leave to dry. Carefully position the burlap (hessian) over the padded mat and glue the raw edges to the back of the board. Leaving a border of burlap ¾ in (18 mm) deep, cut away the center square of burlap. Snip the corners diagonally and glue the inner edges of the fabric to the back of the frame.

Mount your design on the remaining piece of board, gluing the raw edges to the back. Leave to dry. Glue the frame to the front of the design and leave to dry. With a pencil, draw in a moon shape at the top right-hand corner of the picture; go over the outline with the silver glitter pen and then fill in the shape with silver glitter paint.

DMC Flower Threads

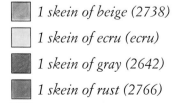

- 1 skein of beige (2738)
- 1 skein of ecru (ecru)
- 1 skein of gray (2642)
- 1 skein of rust (2766)
- 1 skein of brown (2840)

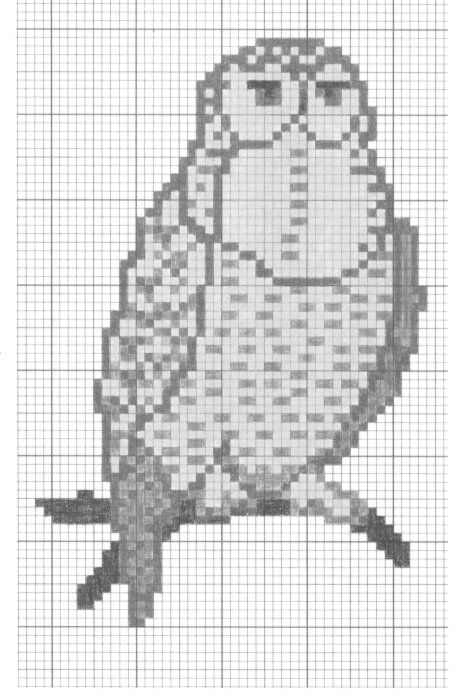

Squirrel Apron

Ready-made gardening aprons are available at garden centers, hardware or department stores. With some waste canvas and a bit of imagination, you can personalize yours with your favorite flowers, or stitch on a friendly squirrel and some nuts, as I have done.

Squirrel design measures:
6 in (15.2 cm) square

Filberts design measures:
1¼ in (3.4 cm) square

Materials
1 heavy cotton gardening apron
No. 8 crewel needle
1 piece of 14-count waste canvas measuring 8½ in (21.6 cm) square
6 pieces of 14-count waste canvas, each measuring 2 in (5 cm) square
Sewing thread for basting
Sewing needle
Pair of tweezers

DMC embroidery floss (cottons)

- ■ 1 skein of dark gray (535)
- ■ 2 skeins of tan (3064)
- ■ 1 skein of gray brown (3032)
- ▢ 1 skein of beige (3045)
- ▢ 1 skein of green (471)
- ▢ 1 skein of light olive (834)
- ■ 1 skein of brown (869)
- ▢ 1 skein of cream (746)
- ▢ 1 skein of pale beige (543)

Instructions

Baste the larger piece of waste canvas to the center of the apron bib. Tack the smaller squares randomly over the pocket. Mark the centers of the charts and the centers of the waste canvas. Starting here, work in cross-stitch using two strands of floss (cotton). When the design is complete, carefully remove the basting stitches, then pull the strands of waste canvas from under the embroidery with the tweezers.

TECHNIQUES

Cross-stitch should be a relaxing and therapeutic pastime, so I have no intention of giving you complicated instructions or baffling you with brilliant finishing techniques. The idea is simply to achieve a neatly worked piece of embroidery without bumps and blemishes and to ensure that all your top stitches slant in the same direction. I have indicated alongside the various projects my own approach to finishing the specific item, but you may prefer to follow your own method.

Material facts

The first thing you must decide is what fabric you are going to stitch on. This will be dictated by the size and purpose of your finished item, the intricacy of the design, and your chosen threads. I have listed here a selection of traditional needlework fabrics, all of which should be available in any good needlecraft store.

Custom-made fabrics

Several fabrics are produced especially for cross-stitch and make life easier for you because the holes in which you stitch are clearly defined. These are great for beginners. In this category I would recommend Aida or Herta. These are brand names for basketweave fabrics which are available in a variety of different counts (stitches per inch), and will enable you to produce a bold and striking pattern or delicate, intricate design with relative ease. The count you select will determine the size of your finished embroidery and will also dictate the thickness of the thread that you can use. The lower the count of the fabric, the fewer stitches per inch it will produce. Herta is widely used in schools and for children's projects because the count is about 6 stitches per inch and it is available in a good range of bright colors. Aida is available in 8-18 count in a choice of subtle colors.

Evenweave fabrics

Needlecraft stores stock a wide range of what are known as evenweave fabrics. "Evenweave" means that there are the same number of horizontal and vertical threads in the materials, making it easy to count the holes and to make your stitches a uniform size. Once again, you will select your fabric according to the count, which is, in this case, determined by the number of threads you work your cross-stitch over.

For example, for fine work you would choose a fabric with a high count and work over one or two threads, while for a bold pattern you would choose a coarser fabric and decide how big you wanted your stitches to be by determining how many threads you were going to work over. Throughout the text in this book, I have referred to the measurement of the canvas as "count," which refers to the number of threads per inch. Place your ruler on a vertical thread of canvas and count how many threads you get in the row for 1 inch. Hardanger and Linda are both attractive evenweave fabrics that can be bought from good needlework stores.

Embroidery linens

These are available in high counts and provide you with a sophisticated background for your work. However, they are expensive, so before selecting them, give consideration to your sight and the time available to you. If you have owlish vision and endless time on your hands, you could produce cross-stitch miniatures by working on silk gauze. This can be purchased pre-mounted in a card frame, but it really needs to be worked through a magnifying glass: eat lots of carrots before beginning.

Plastic canvas

This is particularly popular with children, has a low count, and can be used for three-dimensional projects such as boxes and toys. You should use wool or pearl cotton rather than embroidery floss when working with plastic canvas, and remember that you have to fill your background area completely. Plastic canvas is fun and quick to work with.

Perforated paper

This is a traditional medium which was extremely popular during the Victorian era. It is currently enjoying a revival among stitchers and is used for cutouts and items such as greeting cards, bookmarks, and Christmas decorations.

Canvas

This is normally associated with needlepoint rather than cross-stitch because it is a coarse, stiff fabric. Standard needlepoint canvases consist of an interlocked single thread (mono canvas) or interlocked double threads (double or Penelope canvas). Both varieties are available in a number of different counts. From 10 count down, you should work with wool rather than cotton thread.

Special embroidery fabrics
These are usually sold by the yard, although you will often need only a very small piece for a project such as a greeting card. For this reason, many needlecraft stores sell bags of mixed pieces, which can be good value.

What you will
Any fabric store will offer you a vast range of delights on which to embroider designs, but most general fabrics are plain weave and are often impossible to count. With a little experience, you can safely select cottons with regular patterning such as stripes, ginghams, and damasks, and gauge your stitch positions according to the printed pattern. Do not attempt to use stretchy or knitted fabrics – your work may pucker. Once again, you must take into account the thickness and weight of your intended yarns before you select your material.

Waste not
Waste canvas is a miraculous invention that makes it possible for you to work on a vast range of materials. It is basically a very

TOOLS OF THE TRADE	
If you are a newcomer to cross-stitch you should fill your workbox with the following items:	Pencils (plain and transfer)
	Tracing paper
	A tape measure
Small pieces of evenweave and plain weave fabric (see Material Facts below)	Assorted backing fabrics
	Synthetic batting (polyester wadding)
Assorted threads	
	Ribbons and laces for trimming
Crewel needles (those with large eyes and sharp points)	Rubber cement (rubber glue)
Tapestry needles (those with large eyes and blunt points)	A needle threader
	A pair of tweezers
Sharp scissors	Medium-weight card
Waste canvas (see Material Facts)	An assortment of sewing threads

loosely woven canvas that is available in a selection of counts. To use it, baste it onto the fabric you wish to work on so that it forms an instant grid that defines the size and position of your stitches to the same extent as Aida. Cross-stitch your design in the normal way, unpick the basting stitches, and then pull out the threads of waste canvas from underneath your embroidery with the help of a pair of tweezers. If you pull out all the vertical threads first, you will find that the horizontal threads virtually fall away by themselves. If you have any problem removing these threads, dampen the fabric, and

you will find they are easier to remove.

Thread up
For quality, availability, color, value, and durability, I have worked all my designs using DMC threads, which are available in a staggering choice of colors and qualities. While I have specified particular color numbers, your finished effect will not be spoiled if you go up or down a shade. Six-strand embroidery floss (cotton) goes a long way, especially if you are working on a high-count fabric so, after cross-stitching for only a short time, you are bound to

build up a useful collection of half-used skeins that can be incorporated into future projects.

There is a vast array of threads on the market, and your choice will add to the individuality of your work. I have listed a selection of these below and leave it to you to experiment with the different effects and highlights you can achieve. A major consideration should be that all the threads you use in a single project should be of the same thickness. If you mix thicknesses, you will end up with some skimpy crosses and some fat ones, which will not be a pretty sight – unless, of course, you intend them to look that way.

Six-strand embroidery floss (cotton)
This is sold in small skeins of 8 meters (approximately 26 ft) containing six individual threads. The idea is that you cut a workable length – about 20 in (50 cm) – and split the threads so that you have as many strands as you need for your particular fabric. You can of course mix strands of several colors together to give a subtle shaded effect, and you can buy skeins that are already shaded.

Matte cotton
This is a flat unmercerized thread which works well in bolder designs. It comes in a good choice of colors but does pick up dust

more easily than the slightly shiny varieties. Danish and German flower threads are also flat cottons but are finer. All are spun as a single thread and are not designed to be separated or stranded. They impart a lovely soft quality to your work but do tend to get soiled.

Silks
Stranded cottons are mercerized and therefore have a pleasantly silky luster. However, for the perfectionists among us, there is nothing like the real thing. Silk is available in stranded form and in twisted threads. It is expensive and not very easy to work with because the delicate fibers snag on rough skin. However, the finished effect on very fine work is quite special … reserve it for your masterpiece.

Pearl cottons
Pearl cotton (coton perlé) is a single-twist, high-luster thread that comes in a good selection of colors, including some with a shaded effect. It is available in four different weights, which you choose from according to your background fabric.

Novelty threads
In addition to the above, novelty threads, including a wonderful line of metallics by Kreinik, are constantly being introduced. These can be used to great effect for highlighting details, but be

sure to check that the thickness of the thread is consistent with the basic threads that you have chosen.

Get organized
If you are anything like me, you will always pull the wrong loose end on a skein of thread and end up with a knotted mess that will prove a great joy to your cat. To avoid this, it is a good idea to make yourself a thread organizer before beginning a project. All you need is a small strip of

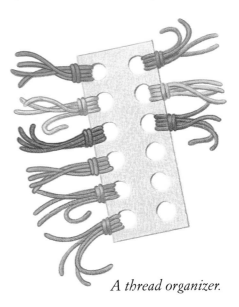

A thread organizer.

lightweight cardboard (an old greeting card is ideal) and a hole punch. Make a hole for each color down the right-hand side of the card and cut your thread into manageable lengths – 20 in (50 cm) is fine. Next to the relevant hole write the color number and, if appropriate, the symbol on the chart, and loop your lengths of thread through it. You can then easily pull out the thread as and when you need it.

Get the needle
To work cross-stitch on evenweave fabrics, use a blunt-tipped tapestry needle. To work using waste canvas you will need a selection of crewel needles. These have sharp points and long, flat eyes so that you can thread a number of strands through at a time without damaging the fabric when you push the needle through. Needles are available in various sizes, and the size you use will depend on the number of threads you are intending to use. A suggested size is given for each project but, as a rule of thumb, work with a needle that feels comfortable and which travels easily through your fabric.

Embroidery frames
When I am working with an evenweave fabric such as Aida, I do not consider it necessary to use a frame. However, I always use a frame when I am stitching on plain weave fabrics or working on a very large project.

There are various types of frame on the market. The most popular for cross-stitch is the hoop, which consists of two concentric circles, one of which is laid under your work and the other laid over your work and then tightened with a screw to hold the fabric taut. It is a good idea to bind both rings with masking tape or cotton tape before beginning because the hoop may mark or distort delicate fabrics.

The other most popular type of frame consists of two parallel dowels with webbing onto which you baste the opposite ends of your fabric. The dowels are then slotted into two straight uprights, which can be tightened to hold the dowels securely. You can rotate the dowels to move the fabric up and down and to keep it taut.

Light up
One miracle of modern science that I would not be without is the daylight bulb. Given that most of us are busy people who only have the evenings available to stitch in, good lighting, especially when you are counting stitches, is essential. Daylight bulbs ease the strain and can be combined with a custom-made magnifying lamp on an adjustable stand, all of which make stitching comfortable and pleasurable. (See Suppliers information on page 166.) You can also buy special holders for your charts and other paraphernalia that will help you get the job done and take the strain out of your work.

Health warning
However much you enjoy or become addicted to your cross-stitch, please don't overdo it. Repetitive strain syndrome is rife among cross-stitchers, and although special wristbands can be purchased to help with this, prevention is better than cure. Work for a couple of hours each evening but then take a break. Make some cookies, walk the dog, or have a deep meaningful conversation with your cat, poodle (or partner) … I know you'd rather be cross-stitching, but you won't be able to do much for weeks on end with a sore arm.

Charts
Many people are frightened of charts, but all you need to remember is that every colored square represents one complete stitch. The heavier lines on the grid are put there to make counting easier for you because each block of squares between the heavy lines represents 10 stitches. Your color key gives you the correct color-coded thread to use so you really cannot go wrong. If you find that you get lost on a chart, the best solution is to take a photocopy of it and cross off the squares as you work them. I work in blocks of color rather than rows, and I keep a number of needles threaded with the different shades of thread so I can change from one to another as necessary.

Sizing the design

For each of the designs in this book, I give the actual size of the motif that you will achieve if you work on my recommended background fabric. However, it is quite easy to re-size the motif by changing the count of the fabric you use. There is a simple formula for working out the size of your design – let's take the marjoram heart design as an example. First, count the number of stitches across at the widest point; on this chart it is 34 stitches. Now count the number of stitches vertically; it is 35 stitches. If you were going to work this design on 28-count linen over two threads, you would need to halve the count to determine the number of stitches to the inch. On 28-count linen you would achieve 14 stitches to the inch. You should now divide the number of stitches on your chart by the number of stitches to the inch – that is (width) 34 stitches divided by 14 = 2.42 in (about 6 cm) by (height) 35 stitches divided by 14 = 2.5 in (about 6 cm).

When you are working on Aida, or over one thread of fabric, do not halve the count before dividing. When calculating how much fabric you need, remember to add at least 1 in (2.5 cm) of extra fabric on all sides of each project to allow for backing or, if it is a picture, for mounting.

If you want to re-size a design

in a major way, your best approach is with a hand-drawn grid. First, trace the outline of your design and draw a squared grid over it. Draw a second grid to the size you require and copy the design square by square from one to the other. Place the enlarged version over a sheet of graph paper and fill in symbols within the traced outlines. This approach should also be used when copying designs from fabric or china.

Charting paper is now available in clear acetate; you can place it over any image that you wish to chart, and fill in the symbols. Alternatively, you can enlarge your design with the use of a photocopier and then re-define the grid by drawing in extra crossed lines to fill in with symbols.

Another method of enlarging is to read every symbol on the chart as a block of four stitches. This in principle will double the size of your design, although you may find it necessary to round off corners by taking away or adding a few stitches to the edges as you work.

Transferring designs

If you do not wish to work with waste canvas, you can easily transfer the image with a water-erasable transfer pencil (available from needlework stores and notions' (haberdashers) departments) and tracing paper.

First, test your fabric by drawing a cross on the tracing paper. Place this face down on the fabric and press it with a warm iron. If this takes to the fabric, you can then trace your complete design and transfer it. There are some wonderful color transfer pens and paints on the market, so you could trace or paint the design in full color and then transfer it to the fabric by ironing it on.

Centering designs

Throughout the book I have suggested that you find the center of the fabric before beginning your embroidery. There are various methods of doing this. If you are using Aida you can count the threads vertically and horizontally and halve the totals to find the center. You could use a tape measure and halve the measurement, or you could fold your fabric both horizontally and vertically to establish the center point. When you are establishing the center point on a piece of fabric that has more selvage on one side than the other, start your count or measurement inside the selvage line.

To find the center of the charts, count the stitches and halve the total. If there is no stitch at the center point, count out to the nearest stitch and start on the equivalent position on your fabric. After establishing your central point, baste a line of stitches both horizontally and vertically on your fabric as a guide. Always work out from the center unless the instructions specify otherwise.

Getting started
Before beginning your work, prevent potential disasters by making sure of the following:
1 Your hands are spotlessly clean and do not smell of garlic. They will need regular washing because fabrics and threads pick up dirt very easily.
2 Your tea or coffee is a safe distance from your work, and that delicious chocolate cake with the gooey icing is not sitting there tempting you to pick it up.
3 The animals have all been instructed not to sit on your lap/shoulder/head and have learned to wipe their paws before coming in from outside and clambering all over you.
4 The children are doing their painting somewhere else – safe, but not within splatter distance of your work area.
5 No one or nothing within reach of you is molting.
6 Your embroidery is not languishing on wet grass.

Stitching
Remember the first rule of cross-stitch – that all the top stitches slant in the same direction. This can be achieved either by working a row of bottom stitches in one

direction and then coming back along the row in the opposite direction or by working each complete cross individually. Both these methods are perfectly acceptable, but the option you choose should depend on how many stitches you have in a row before the color changes. You can work in any direction, but always insert your needle after the correct number of threads in your background material. The

Cross-stitch on plain weave fabric.

Cross-stitch evenweave fabric (Aida)

diagrams show a cross-stitch being worked over two threads on simple evenweave fabric and on a basketweave fabric such as Aida. It is a good idea to thread several needles with different colors before you begin. Use a needle-threader – it will save your sight and your time.

Cross-stitch is the only stitch you will need to master to complete the majority of projects in this book. However, one or two of the designs require additional stitches. When I refer to straight stitch I mean exactly that: small backstitches worked in a row, the same size as a half cross-stitch. Half stitch is as it sounds: work the first half of a cross-stitch only, i.e, do not go back to complete the full cross.

Stretching
I did not find it necessary to block any of the projects in this book. However, if you do find the shape of your work is slightly distorted, place it face down on a blocking board, which you should cover with clean paper or a sheet, and pull it into shape by inserting rustproof tacks at 1 in (2.5 cm) intervals. Dampen your work thoroughly with a clean sponge, or spray and leave it to dry.

Framing
Because cross-stitch fabric is very soft, it is usually quite simple when you are framing projects to

stretch your finished work into shape on a backing board. Either glue the work into position using rubber cement (glue) or, using strong string, lace it across the back in criss-cross fashion until it is taut (see diagram).

Before using either of these methods, center your finished work on your board. Insert pins, starting with the four corners, and then spaced at 1 in (2.5 cm) intervals all around the edge of the needlework and board to make sure the work is straight and undistorted. You can then add a decorative front or frame it as you please. Finished pieces intended for book covers and folders can be pulled into shape during the finishing process. When mounting a piece of embroidery, use acid-free board to ensure it remains in good condition for the generations ahead of you who will treasure your work.

Trimmings

I hope this book has given you lots of new ideas for uses of your cross-stitch projects. Most craft people are, by nature, collectors, and I would expect you to have a basket or box of fabric pieces and furnishing trims. Use whatever you like to make a project, but consider the weight of any fabric you intend to be sure it is compatible with the fabric you have stitched on. In a couple of projects I have used twisted cords; to make a twisted cord, hold several strands of thread together and tie one end to something solid. Repeatedly twist this length of thread until it is tight and then, keeping the twist, unfasten the tied end. Hold both ends together and let the doubled thread twist around itself. Secure at both ends.

Care

However careful you are, accidents inevitably happen, but if you have used the recommended threads you should have no problem repairing the damage. Before washing a piece of embroidery always check the colorfastness of the thread and fabric you have used, and follow the manufacturer's directions. DMC and Anchor threads are reputed to be fast-dyed and can be machine-washed at 96°F (35°C), but you must also take the directions for washing the background fabric into account. As a general rule, always avoid bleach and harsh detergents and do not tumble-dry.

When you iron your work, place it facedown over a fluffy towel to prevent any flattening of the stitches. Then steam-press or use a damp cloth, ironing on the wrong side of the work only.

To frame cross-stitch, center the finished work on a sheet of cardboard and insert pins all the way around at 1-inch (2.5 cm) intervals. Then either glue into position or lace it across the back with heavy thread, as shown here.

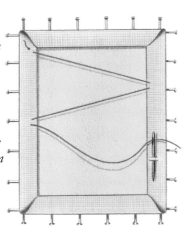
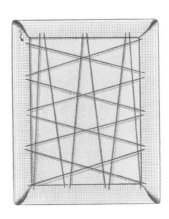

Suppliers Information

UNITED STATES

The project directions in this book call for materials that are widely available in craft stores. If you have difficulty locating specific items, contact the manufacturers or distributors listed below to find sources in your area.

For cotton and lace-trimmed items similar to those available from the author (left), contact:

Peking Handicraft, Inc.
1388 San Mateo Avenue
South San Francisco, CA 94080

For a free catalog of clock dials, hands, and quartz movements, as well as barometers and thermometers, contact:

Klockit
P.O. Box 636
Dept. CSG5
Lake Geneva, WI 53147
(800) 556-2548 (KLOCKIT)

For information about the Framecraft/Anne Brinkley Designs pillboxes, jars, bellpull hangers, and all manner of wonderful gift items for cross-stitching, contact:

Stitchworks
1502 21st Street NW
Washington, DC 20036
(800) 558-WOOL

and
Gay Bowles Sales
P.O. Box 1060
Janesville, WI 53547
(800) 447-1332

The floss used in this book was kindly supplied by DMC. To order, contact:

Herrschners Inc.
2800 Hoover Road
Stevens Point, WI 54481
(800) 441-0838

For information about Anchor threads, contact:

Anchor/Marlitt Floss
Coats & Clark, Inc.
Consumer Service Dept.
P.O. Box 27067
Greenville, SC 29616

For information about Kreinik threads, contact:

Kreinik Manufacture
P.O. Box 1966
Parkersburg, WV 26102
(800) 624-1928

To order Zweigart evenweave fabric, contact:

Rosemary Drysdale
80 Long Lane
East Hampton, NY 11937
(516) 324-1705

Acknowledgments

A book of this kind is dependent on joint effort, generosity, painstaking hard work, and moral support. The team who worked on this book are second to none, and my sincere thanks go out to the following individuals and companies.

For making this book possible through their excellent and endless stitching:
Carolyn Palmer, Anne Peterson, Valerie Clark, Freda Brown, Jane Fox, Mary Baker, Joan Firmin, Clare Powderly, Kristine Evans, Carol Edwards, Lucy Payne, Lynn Gensberg, and Josie Hyde.

For turning the needlework into treasures:
Jeanette Hall.

For the beautiful styling and photographs:
Jon and Barbara Stewart.

For keeping my nose to the grindstone, my editors:
Jane Donovan, Kate Yeates, and Jane Struthers.

For encouragement, support and money:
Carey Smith, Colin Gower, and Colin Ancliffe.

For keeping me supplied with endless cups of tea:
Pat Groves.

For excellent yarns, fabrics, and service:
DMC, especially Cara Ackerman.

For "Cross-Stitch Master", the best little cross-stitch computer program on the market:
Jeff Tullin of Ursa Software, 17 Camborne Grove, Gateshead, Tyne and Wear, NE8 4EX, United Kingdom.

For an excellent framing and stretching service:
Anne Gillis, Darkgate, Carmarthen, Dyfed.

DMC/Anchor Conversion Chart

DMC	Anchor	DMC	Anchor	DMC	Anchor	DMC	Anchor	DMC	Anchor	DMC	Anchor	DMC	Anchor
blanc	1	353	6	550	102	720	326	809	130	951	1010	3326	36
223	895	367	217	552	99	725	305	817	13	956	40	3346	267
224	893	368	214	553	98	727	293	830	277	957	50	3347	266
300	352	414	235	554	96	729	890	832	907	958	187	3348	264
307	289	415	398	561	212	740	316	834	874	966	206	3364	260
309	42	433	358	562	210	741	304	839	360	972	298	3371	382
310	403	436	1045	564	206	742	303	869	944	977	1002	3708	31
317	400	437	362	580	281	743	302	891	35	3012	844	3716	25
320	215	444	290	597	168	744	301	893	28	3032	903	3721	896
326	59	451	233	602	63	746	275	906	256	3033	391	3743	869
333	119	453	231	606	334	754	1012	907	255	3041	871	3782	899
335	38	469	267	632	936	762	234	921	1003	3042	870	3790	393
340	118	470	267	666	46	792	941	922	1003	3045	888		
349	13	471	266	676	891	793	176	934	862	3047	852		
351	10	535	1041	677	886	794	175	936	269	3064	883		
352	9	543	933	700	228	801	359	945	881	3325	129		

Index